ENDORSE

We all have the option of becoming strong at the broken places, but I believe it makes more sense to learn from the wisdom of those who have preceded us. *Spiritual Engineering*'s content is an excellent guide to healing your life.

—Bernie Siegel, MD,
Bestselling author of *365 Prescriptions for the Soul;
Love, Medicine, and Miracles; and
Faith, Hope & Healing*

Exciting, controversial, inspiring, and comforting. Tom's challenges the foundation of this culture's deep beliefs. A man with a powerful message.

—Simone Mason
Recipient of the National Athena Award and host of
"Faith in Action" 1340 AM, WYBC

Tom's simple procedure for teaching people how not to worry is a godsend. His enthusiasm and his energy motivates listeners.

—Dr. Winn Henderson
Critically acclaimed and author of *Share Your Mission*
International and talk show host

Tom has done something different, even a little courageous—combining psychology with down-to-earth spirituality. Not a chance I would have bought into anything fanatical or unbelievable. Nor did I wish to plow through a bunch of psychological jargon. Simple guidance and reassurance day or night. The power to relieve emotional misery right now.

—Kevin R. Systems
Analyst, Corpus Christi, Texas

I very quickly realized that this material produces a breakthrough in the logical thinking, while soothing the human spirit with its calming effect. Your technique to achieve peace of mind is presented in a clever, systematic, practical, yet insightful manner.

—Patricia Spratling
Parent Educator, Fort Lauderdale, Florida

I was very sad for many years. Went to church but nothing made me feel better. Thomas's teaching changed my life completely. Very soon I got big happy inside. Thank you.

—Sue Jayaralne
Housekeeper, Kandy, Sri Lanka

Your teachings touched my heart. It really works; I have never met anyone who could blend in both psychology and faith that well. It just amazed me! Thank you for doing this for me and millions of others.

—Jack Liu
Beijing China

SPIRITUAL
ENGINEERING

SPIRITUAL ENGINEERING

THOMAS J. STRAWSER

TATE PUBLISHING
AND ENTERPRISES, LLC

Published by Tate Publishing & Enterprises, LLC
127 E. Trade Center Terrace | Mustang, Oklahoma 73064 USA
1.888.361.9473 | www.tatepublishing.com

Tate Publishing is committed to excellence in the publishing industry. The company reflects the philosophy established by the founders, based on Psalm 68:11,
"The Lord gave the word and great was the company of those who published it."

Book design copyright © 2014 by Tate Publishing, LLC. All rights reserved.
Cover design by Jim Villaflores
Cover logo design by Spiritual Engineering INC
Interior design by Mary Jean Archival

Published in the United States of America
ISBN: 978-1-63063-276-2
1. Self-Help / General
2. Self-Help / Spiritual
14.03.25

Dedication

I dedicate this to all my spiritual helpers, especially the women who contributed to my spiritual growth. The spiritual giants emblazoned on the pages of history are often men; however, women often act as the spiritual torchbearers, quietly and inexorably lighting the path that guides humanity forward in the true and meaningful values of living. To my great fortune, many such women have blessed my life. My mother Mary, a loving, wise, and gentle person, taught me values and principles, demonstrated the power resulting from an unassuming spiritual life and encouraged an early freedom to explore for God; my late wife Barbara stood beside me in my darkest times and faced an oncoming and certain death with poise, peace, and courage; and Berkeley Elliot, an outspoken and loving spiritual mentor, expanded my concepts of God and life.

Finally, I express my gratitude to my wife Patricia, a true spiritual companion and partner. She is my cheerleader, advocate, loving critic, and *amor de mi vida* (love of my life) who lit a fire of love within me during the first hours of our meeting, a love that shall never extinguish or grow dim. Miss Patty demonstrates a profound and awesome ability to unify her life with these concepts and constantly challenges me to live these principles—to *walk the walk*. Sharing our lives, supporting each other in our individual and partner growth, and helping other people experience the transforming embrace of a practical spirituality has blessed me with a life beyond my wildest dreams.

Reviews

With a rocketing divorce rate, could there be a flaw in the spirit of society? Spiritual Engineering brings an intriguing collection of thoughts to the table encouraging a self-reevaluation of thoughts, belief, and self-acceptance. Encouraging readers to bring stronger relationships and keep the negative emotions out of their lives, Spiritual Engineering comes to readers with plenty of thought and encouragement to lead a more spiritual and fulfilling life.

—Midwest Book Review, Volume 9, Number 10

Finally an author that has used a rational, logical approach—in, fact an engineer's approach—to applying the techniques and processes that we need to reach our spiritual core, our own happiness.

Spiritual Engineering is complete, concise, and extremely detailed—a most valuable tool for everyone regardless of your emotional maturity, self-knowledge, or need to improve your relationships. Learn to love yourself first and then love others completely and without fear.

—All Books Review

Acknowledgements

Many of the original sources and works contributing to the development of *Spiritual Engineering* concepts and techniques are acknowledged throughout this book. However, I want to make a special recognition to Patricia Strawser.

Patricia's artistic abilities, spiritual commitment, and probing intellect helped shape *Spiritual Engineering*.

She is responsible for all the drawings in this book and her ability to convey my ideas with a drawing is exemplified by the front cover logo. When asked to develop a single picture that epitomized these innovative concepts, she immediately drew the portrayal of a person existing with relationships, feelings, mind, and science revolving around a God-centered life. She raised questions, suggested ideas, and offered loving criticism that elevated this work to a higher level. Patricia did the primary translating to make this work available in Spanish. I am blessed to have such a partner that is truly the cofounder and the mother of *Spiritual Engineering*.

Contents

Introduction

This is a book about spirituality, but it's unlike most books you will find on this topic. For starters, you don't have to come to it as a believer. I've had the honor of presenting spiritual engineering concepts to thousands of people around the world and among the enthusiastic proponents of this program have been Buddhists, Muslims, Christians, and Hindus, as well as many who came to it as questioning believers and agnostics.

I avoided spirituality for many years because it didn't fit with the way I saw life. I was an engineer, married to logic, and was certain I could surmount any obstacle with hard work, determination, and my scientific approach. But I hit a time when these could not provide real solutions with feelings and relationships and came within a hairs-breath of suicide.

I simply wanted to be happy. So I did vast amounts of research on what really worked to help people enjoy some happiness. To my surprise, I discovered overwhelming evidence that people with certain spiritual concepts and practices simply experienced a better life than others. But I was not ready to lay aside science and logic. I knew there must be a way to harmonize modern knowledge with a spiritual life.

As an engineer, I work with energy—force—power. I was astounded to discover that each of us possesses a very real spiritual energy, an inner raw power that can dramatically transform our lives. Very few people ever discover this internal energy or learn the skills that allow it to help them. This book describes the process of Spiritual Engineering that helps you do exactly that.

This method integrates engineering, science, psychology, and personal spirituality in an innovative approach. It is different from many religions or other spiritual paths. *Spiritual Engineering* centers on cause and effect, action and results. Instead of saying, "Believe what we tell you, act in line with that belief, and you'll reap the rewards," you are invited to be a little open-minded and work through the process—to experiment with new behaviors and thought patterns, experience the results, and then develop your own beliefs based on those results.

So we're going to talk about science and use the scientific process, but don't worry if you don't have a scientific bone in your body—this doesn't require a smidgen of math! We'll just see how many of the rules that describe our natural world also apply—remarkably well—to our feelings and relationships.

For example, electricity helped me begin to understand this spiritual power that lies dormant within each of us, the power that propels the personal transformation. Everyone in the developed world believes that electricity exists. Why? We can't see it. We can only see how the power of electricity affects different objects. This unseen energy flows into our homes and behind the walls until we choose to use it. We flip a switch and the light comes on. The light bulb is just a piece of glass and filament until it accesses the electrical power; then it dramatically changes. It's still a light bulb, but the flow of unseen energy has helped it accomplish its intended purpose—to produce light.

We accept electricity and other forces because we observe their effects on objects. That's how many have come to understand this spiritual force within us. You don't have to be an electrical engineer to benefit from electricity; you just have to connect the need (the lamp) with the source of energy. Nor do you have to understand theology to access the spiritual power that is flowing inside you right now. But, like electricity, you have to make the connection to see the power work.

Those who have wholeheartedly entered into this process have found that it opens doors to the highest-quality life possible—the best relationships, the most profound happiness, and the ability to face any problem or adversity in life without fear. Lofty claims, to be sure. But as you will see, if you follow the process and do the work, these claims will be borne out in your own personal experiences. It's not magic. It's like baking a cake—*Spiritual Engineering* provides the recipe. You follow it and do the work—and you get the cake every time! What you believe makes no difference at all.

We can live our entire life on this planet without any spiritual belief. My research concluded that this yields an existence of coping, just getting by, and struggle. We feel like something is missing. Life should, and can be, much more than this. The solution is to acquire a spirituality that grounds us in values, principles, ideals, and purpose. If you avoid this the way I used to, consider this: Are you open-minded enough to suspend your preconceptions and try a few simple experiments that may improve your life?

PART ONE

Discovering the Common Threads Connecting Spirituality, Science, Feelings, and Relationships

The Climax of Emotional Misery: Suicide Is an Option

"The greatest affliction in life is never to be afflicted. Men only learn wisdom by experiencing tribulations."

—*The Urantia Book*

I lay in bed in a decrepit one-bedroom apartment, crying as I stared at the cracked ceiling. At the ripe old age of thirty-three, my life was over. I had lost all I valued in life, with no hope of ever reclaiming it. The truth had sunk in—my home was broken, my dreams of being with my children were shattered, and my business was almost ruined. My wife had filed for divorce. I felt totally worthless as a man, a husband, and a human being.

My chest felt as though a boa constrictor were squeezing me in a death grip. Each breath required an effort; I just could not get enough air. Dark, dismal, dirty, and decrepit described both the apartment and my soul. I never knew a man could feel so low, so utterly hopeless and helpless. Gut-wrenching sobs racked my body. I had not known it was possible to hurt this much.

For three years, our marriage had decayed from occasional arguments into constant fighting. Counseling, religion, and self-help manuals had not provided any answers. I discovered relief only through chemicals—first using a prescribed medicine and then turning to alcohol.

I had moved into this small apartment to await the final divorce proceedings. I could have afforded a better place, but it seemed appropriate that my surroundings match the ugliness of my feelings. I didn't know what to do. I couldn't find anything that would relieve the misery. Both my mother and my childhood church had taught me about a benevolent God that intervened in the affairs of man, but I had sacrificed these early beliefs to a scientific approach to life. Now this logical training failed to provide answers for my emotional turmoil or give any hope that I could ever find real solutions. I told myself over and over that I needed to let it go and move on. Move on. Right. I could barely make it from the bed to the toilet.

Nighttime multiplied the mental torture. Throughout the cold, dark, rainy hours, a sense of total hopelessness swirled through the witches' brew in my mind. Each thought about how unfair this all was and how badly I had been treated led to more of the same. My lament, *Now, I can't be a real father to my children*, turned to resentment and bitterness, *Why can't she change? Can't she see what she's doing?* and then moved to *I know I've made mistakes, but my God, I don't want this.* Then I'd take a drink of scotch to ease the pain and clear my thinking—or so I thought.

My emotions sank lower with each passing moment. I knew I couldn't take it much longer, but I couldn't break free either. I thought of the father I had never known, the man who had committed suicide when I was two years old. I had always thought his final act had been despicable, selfish, and cowardly. My judgment of him—and of many other people and things—reflected the pride of the self-sufficient engineer who believed that he could achieve anything. Now I understood what my father had felt.

I lay in the dirty, rumpled bed, desperately pleading with a God that I did not believe would ever help me, to please relieve my pain. I had long since given up any belief that this entity I called God would do anything for me, but I had nothing else left to try. As expected, nothing happened. I walked to the one chair in my apartment and sat down. I picked up the fifth of scotch and saw that I had enough left to put me out again. I choked down another big hit, but it barely fazed me. Filled with self-pity as I looked at the peeling linoleum, the unmade bed and dirty dishes, tears started rolling down again. How had I ended up here?

I made a decision. I had hurt long enough. I picked up the .357 revolver and jammed the barrel deep in my mouth, feeling the front sight digging into flesh and drawing blood. The 150-grain bullets would make an exit hole the size of my fist. I would have no chance to second-guess this one. I pulled slack out of the trigger, knowing exactly how much tension this trigger required to drop the hammer. With a scant sixteenth of an inch of trigger-pull left, a thought flashed into my mind, *Hey! Wait a minute. You can always do this later if things don't get better.*

This small thought, though it hardly seemed profound, penetrated the alcohol haze like a laser through smoke. Somehow, this simple interruption allowed me to make a different choice. Knowing that if I couldn't find a way out I could always return and pull that trigger gave me a choice that I could accept, at least for the moment. In retrospect, that specific thought was probably the only thought that could have stopped me from pulling the trigger. If it would have been, *You'll go to hell if you do this,* or something similar, I would have finished the sequence.

I didn't know it then, but later I understood that sometimes the spiritual power that resides within every human being, whether we call it God, Supreme Being, Great Spirit, or another name often works this way. No flash of light, no burning bush but simply a quiet thought, a subtle shift in attitude.

When I got up the next day, I made myself go out for lunch. I forced down a few bites. The restaurant was bright and bustling with activity. I sat there drinking ice water, relieved to be out of my miserable apartment. I reflected on the night before, and the realization of how close I had come to a self-inflicted death terrified me. The overwhelming emotional agony had made suicide a seemingly reasonable option. I was scared now because I had only promised myself time to think, and I was almost certain

I would return to the idea of killing myself if I couldn't find a better way to live.

I thought again of my father, but this time I considered how much pain his single, desperate act had cost our family and me. I knew exactly how a small boy feels growing up without a father. I had no one to teach me how to fish, how to shave, how to talk to girls, or drive a car. These memories led me to hope that I would keep trying to find a reason to live, as long as the smallest chance existed for sharing with my own children the things I'd missed out on because of my father's fateful choice.

But how? I just wanted to be able to live and not hurt so much. Why couldn't someone give me a solution? I'd already exhausted every option I could think of for improving my life. Were the numbing effects of drugs and alcohol, or even the oblivion of suicide, all that was left to me?

As I tried to think my situation through one last time, another one of those thoughts from nowhere sprang into my tired mind, *I'm an engineer. I solve problems for a living. Why can't I use my engineering skills to solve problems with feelings?* With that thought, the answer became obvious—the scientific process was the key to solving problems! I just needed to use the same logical, proven methods I would apply to a multifaceted engineering problem to solve my emotional problems. Now I had a goal, and I had a method that might get me to that goal.

Emerging from my near suicide, I had one simple but very clear insight: I should never make long-term decisions based on short-term pain. It became frighteningly apparent that the emotional pain I felt in any given moment could, and did, distort my decision-making abilities. Beyond that basic understanding, all I had were questions. Could I really use engineering methods to find solutions for emotional problems? Could scientific principles help identify solutions for my problems with difficult feelings and relationships? My gut told me that I was sitting on something important, but I could not yet see where all this was going.

Starting out of the Darkness:
A Glimmer of Hope

"He who has felt the deepest grief is best able to experience supreme happiness. We must have felt what it is to die, that we may appreciate the enjoyments of life."

—Alexander Dumas

If anything positive can be said about reaching such a low point, it's that you truly have nothing to lose. That perspective allowed me to open my eyes to my situation. I realized that, for better or worse, my emotional responses and relationships were classic examples of Isaac Newton's first law of motion. This gave me the first concrete clue that scientific principles might well apply to the aspects of my life that, until then, had seemed mysterious and unknowable.

"A body at rest tends to stay at rest, and a body in motion tends to stay in motion with the same speed and in the same direction unless acted upon by an external force."

—Isaac Newton (Newton's first law of motion)

Applying this law to my feelings and relationships revealed that, if I kept doing what I'd been doing, I'd keep getting what I'd been getting. If I kept heading in the same direction, I would stay on the same path and keep feeling the same way I'd been feeling.

Or *if nothing changes, nothing changes*. If I wanted to change my life, I would have to do something different. I had to move in a different direction.

It's funny now as I remember how excited I was that I had found a logical principle that applied to my emotions. This was the first of many physical laws that I was able to apply to feelings and relationships.

Spiritual Engineering Axiom #1

If nothing changes,
nothing changes

Now, I'd love to report that I traded all my misery for this new life overnight, but that didn't happen. Despite my big breakthrough, I slipped into full-blown alcoholism. I had progressed so far into the physical and psychological patterns of addiction that I did not simply *turn it around* because of this insight. Feelings of anger, guilt, remorse, fear, uselessness, and hopelessness controlled me. I was certain that my scientific approach held solutions, but alcohol continued to be my answer for misery.

I descended into a living hell where my body and mind needed alcohol to survive—to get through the day, or through the next hour. I drank when I didn't want to drink; when I was consciously ashamed of the very act I was committing; when I knew that I was slowly killing myself. Countless times I drank to oblivion, yet I somehow remained conscious enough to feel the depths of shame and guilt. Sobering up the next morning, I couldn't look at myself in a mirror. I'd have to take more alcohol to stop the shakes and tremors. I showered often and kept cologne and breath spray in my pocket so no one could smell the decadence I knew I exuded.

I went into treatment for alcoholism, but strongly resisted the truth that I was an alcoholic. I thought I was too smart, too educated, and too strong-willed. But that was delusion. Each time I drank, I slipped farther down into that bottomless pit until I could no longer refute the overwhelming evidence.

Finally, I totally surrendered and made a wholehearted commitment to follow the recovery program exactly as designed—with no shortcuts. As my mind began to clear, I remembered my plan to use engineering and science to find answers for a better life. For over twenty-five years, I poured myself into everything that I imagined might lead to solid, practical solutions. I went back to school and got a master's degree in psychology, studied different religions and investigated numerous self-help programs. I focused on finding a process, a recipe, for happiness and wonderful relationships.

My investigation led me to conclude that no single field or religion holds the secret. Instead, I discovered that a variety of groups had found a way to be happy in spite of severe problems and chaos. The engineering techniques identified similarities among these divergent groups, and they also formulated the process by which the individuals in each group had achieved their personal transformation.

Having a step-by-step procedure greatly decreases the time and effort it takes to solve any problem. It's like baking a cake. When you have the recipe, all you have to do is gather the ingredients, follow directions, do some work, and you get a great cake. It's not magic or something that only works once in a while—it's dependable.

Recognizing the process came quickly but breaking it into simple, straightforward guidelines took considerably longer. Through trial and error, consistent practice, and input from people practicing the techniques, the process of *Spiritual Engineering* evolved.

These solutions simply work. Ever since I learned to apply them, I've had a fantastic life, in spite of life's problems and numerous painful losses. Most of the time, these tools keep me free of worry, fear, and misery—no matter what is happening in the world around me. They taught me skills that helped me build an intimate relationship with a woman that transcends anything I ever thought was possible.

I still have days when I'm down, and I still experience pain. I hurt and cry sometimes. But the depth and frequency of fear, worry, chaos, and confusion are much less than before. Now I can choose between having a bad five minutes or a bad day. No matter what happens, I have complete confidence that I have solutions that work for any problem life can throw at me. And experience has shown that they work for anyone who wants to break the shackles of misery—anyone who is open-minded and willing to do the work.

Every time I recall the low point I reached before coming to this understanding, I'm humbled to think that, had I pulled the trigger, none of this could ever have happened.

Searching for the Solution:
Applying Engineering Principles to Feelings and Relationships

"Life is just a bowl of pits."

—Rodney Dangerfield

B efore becoming an emotional cripple, almost committing suicide, and sinking into alcoholism, I had thought everyone should be able to control feelings with their minds and their willpower. This was great in theory, but the results left a lot to be desired. My experience proved that my mind could not always control my feelings, but I realized that my logical thinking process might give me some tools that could shape the emotional part of my life.

The Engineering Process

In my work as an engineer, I had developed a systematic two-part process for solving problems. In applying this technique to emotions, I defined a personal problem as any situation or event that directly threatens my personal well-being. Simple and straightforward. Then I applied the systematic process for tackling complex problems to my feelings and relationships. I needed answers.

The Engineering Problem-Solving Technique

Part One: Differentiation or Eliminating Non-Problems

1. Is this really a problem?
2. Is it my responsibility to solve it?
3. Can I do anything about it today?
4. Do I really want to solve this?

Part Two: Finding and Maintaining a Solution

1. Accept and process the problem.
   Separate problem from symptoms.
   Find the root cause.
2. Evaluate possible solutions.
3. Identify the best solution.
4. Implement this solution.
5. Perform the necessary maintenance.

People waste a lot of time and energy on issues that aren't really problems. Differentiation separates non-problems from real problems and thereby allows us to focus on solving the real problems. Focusing our energy this way leads to more effective solutions. To see how this differentiation technique applies to personal problems, here are some questions we might ask ourselves about our perceived problem:

Personal Differentiation Process

- Is it really a problem, or is it something I think might be a problem? Is it a *direct and immediate threat* to my well-being, or is it just a nuisance, an irritation? Am I just reacting?
- Is it my responsibility? Whose decisions and actions have brought about this problem? Am I protecting someone

else from the consequences of his or her choices or actions? If I take no action will the outcome cause me direct harm? Will it cause someone else harm? If so, why do I have an obligation to prevent it? Is this any of my business?

- Can I do anything about it today that will prevent or alter the situation? If I *can* take an action today, I need to do so and then move on. If I cannot take an action on it today, it's not a problem today. It may become an immediate and direct threat tomorrow but it isn't today. Instead, it's a worry, an illusionary problem.
- Do I really need to solve it? Sometimes we forget that we don't have to find a *solution* for every problem we face.
- How big is it really? Am I blowing this out of proportion and over-reacting? Many current upsets have little long-term impact on our lives.

In my own life, differentiation made it obvious that I had a concrete problem. Putting a gun in my mouth and almost committing suicide definitely qualified as a problem. That led me to the second part of this technique.

Applying Step 1 of "Finding a Solution" to my emotions and relationships uncovered another revelation. This engineering approach offers a root cause analysis (RCA) to methodically eliminate symptoms and secondary problems until only the root cause remains. This primal cause constitutes the *one* thing that *must* be changed to prevent a recurrence of the failure. It's the first domino that starts the entire stack falling.

The RCA quickly made it obvious that my fear, anger, guilt, worry, and other forms of misery were only symptoms—not the real problems. This was a major insight. I knew that working on symptoms rarely solved the underlying problem. Carrying the analysis further showed me the primal cause of my emotional misery. *Most of these symptoms originated from decisions I made.* In some cases, events and other people contributed to the problem, but very often, my own decisions and reactions were the real source of my contention. At some point in the immediate or distant past, I had made a choice that put me in a position to later feel some type of misery. The solution was obvious, I needed to make better choices. However, this analysis also showed, unequivocally, that I lacked the skills to make such choices. In honestly looking at my past history, I saw that I always thought my decision—at the moment it was made—was the best choice. I obviously needed new decision-making skills.

But which skills, and how was I to acquire them? Steps 2 and 3 of "Finding a Solution" focused my efforts on finding *proven, verifiable results that had worked for others with similar problems.* Then, I could develop a process that would let me achieve those results in my own life.

The beginning of this objective investigation illuminated three startling facts about feelings and relationships in our world today.

1. Millions of people are suffering.
2. Current approaches are failing.
3. Some people have discovered answers.

Millions Are Suffering

When you say you've had a great or terrible day, you're referring to how you *felt* that day. Feelings define our quality of life. They range from gut-wrenching, palm-sweating, stay-awake–at-night misery to exuberant joy and happiness. Yet statistics clearly indicate that, for many of us, negative feelings far outweigh positive ones, leading to anxiety and stress, drug and alcohol abuse, and poor health. These emotions originate and find expression in relationships. We're not doing well in this area. In the United States alone, for example:

- Forty-eight percent of first-time marriages, 67 percent of second marriages, and 73 percent of third marriages end in divorce [1]
- Nearly 50 million people have experienced divorce [2]
- Seventy-five percent of doctor visits are stress-related [3]
- Forty million people suffer from anxiety [4]
- Forty-three million people abuse alcohol or prescription drugs, or use illegal drugs [5]
- Forty-eight million smoke after knowing the risks involved [5]
- More than 100 million people in United States are obese.[6]

Wow! When it's all put together like this, we get a true picture of the current state of humanity. It's a pretty sad image.

For many people, marriage is the primary relationship in their life. More time, emotion, and energy are invested in making marriages succeed than in any other relationships. Despite this, almost 50 percent of marriages disintegrate. They fail to fulfill the hopes or achieve the promises of the wedding day. This doesn't include the millions who remain married in unfulfilled and stagnated relationships—those who settle for less than their dreams.

These same statistics reveal another startling fact: There's a significantly higher failure rate with second and third marriages than there is with initial partnerships. Of course, the extra complications in these second unions help us rationalize these numbers; however, one inescapable question arises from such justification: *If we learned from the initial marriage failures, shouldn't we expect our success rate to increase rather than get worse?* Should we not learn how to select a more compatible mate? How to allow disagreements to become a process for growth? How to love but not enable? How to build healthy relationships? If our best efforts fail this badly, where does that leave the other relationships in our lives?

Current Approaches Are Failing

Where do we go for help when emotional miseries upset our lives or when our relationships are troubled? Some try chemicals to solve the problem. Alcohol and drugs let them feel better for a short time, help them socialize or relax, take the edge off reality and make it more bearable. But the misery returns and more chemicals are required.

Others reinforce their dependence on materialism. People acquire money, cars, houses, jobs, fame, golf club memberships, power, accomplishments, or that slim physique in order to feel better. Attaining the goal yields a short-term satisfaction, but it never addresses the underlying problem. Like chemical dependency, materialism requires acquiring more and more to ease that inner discontent, but misery always returns.

Many people find answers in counseling, psychology, and religion that help them enjoy life; however, millions of others try these and fail to find rewarding solutions. Some discover partial answers that help them survive or cope, but they cannot claim true happiness or peace of mind. Something is missing. Anxiety, worry, guilt, anger, envy, jealousy, and other emotional miseries still plague their days and nights.

The statistics are irrefutable. Our emotions remain in chaos. Our relationships continue to disintegrate, and misery permeates our existence. All this occurs in spite of the help delivered by caring professionals and organizations. In spite of our efforts, we are not solving the problem.

Misery is sneaky and progressive. We don't feel wonderful and then suddenly awaken one morning with the weight of the world pressing us down. Instead, we *slowly* accept that feeling bad is normal. It's like living in a manure pile and not realizing how bad it smells until we get out of it. Psychologists use the *Fassell analogy* to describe this phenomenon:

"If you drop a frog into a pot of boiling water, it will hop out immediately. But if you put the frog into a pot of cool water and then slowly heat the water to boiling, the frog will stay there until it dies."

We cope, we survive, and we hurt. We accept the ever-increasing misery as being normal. But we don't have to accept this condition. Misery is optional—and self-inflicted.

Discovering the Answers

My extensive research didn't uncover only bad news. Some people had found secrets to a genuinely happier life. Leading psychologists and psychiatrists across the last century studied many of these people. In 1902, William James, the father of American psychology, wrote about people whom he referred to as the *twice-born* people. All of these people had undergone a *spiritual experience* and then "changed from a state of tenseness, worry, selfishness, and morbid melancholy to one of calmness, receptivity, and peace—reflecting a paradise of inner tranquility and a feeling of safety." [7]

A few decades later, Carl Jung, the Swiss psychiatrist, reported that through a *religious experience* certain people learned to cope with unpleasant life situations; they could calmly face circumstances that would drive others to suicide.

In the mid-twentieth century, psychologist Abraham Maslow introduced the concept of self-actualizing people whom he called the *apex of human development.* He estimated that less than one percent of humanity ever achieved this level. All of the self-actualizers had undergone a profound inner transformation that he called a *peak experience.* These people

* were no longer afraid of the unknown;
* accepted themselves, others, and nature;
* felt no shame or guilt about their human frailties;

- lived in the moment, free of past and future concerns;
- were not self-centered;
- did not depend on outside circumstances or other people for their satisfactions or sense of personal value;
- experienced awe, pleasure, and wonder in their everyday world. [8,9]

As my research brought me through the rest of the twentieth century, I realized that these amazing experiences are not limited to people in the past. Some surprising groups demonstrated results similar to those recorded by the professionals. The original twelve-step program, Alcoholics Anonymous (AA), provides guidelines to achieve a *spiritual awakening* that modifies the alcoholic's thinking patterns and alters years of destructive behavior. This program emphasizes that stopping drinking is the initial and primary benefit, but it also underscores that a spiritual power can yield dramatic quality-of-life improvements far beyond this first reward.

I talked with hundreds of participants in AA and other twelve-step programs. Many entered the program and were content with physical sobriety because it was such a tremendous improvement over their former lives. However, others went the extra mile and actively engaged in the spiritual process outlined by the AA program. Many of these people demonstrated attributes that were identical to those described by Maslow in self-actualizing people.

Narcotics Anonymous, Overeaters Anonymous, Emotions Anonymous, Sex Anonymous, and more than forty similar groups use these twelve steps to combat their specific addiction. This twelve-step solution relieves a variety of symptoms because it attacks the problem's root cause, offers a specific process to achieve the results, and provides maintenance to make the results continuous. This is a universal solution; therefore, it's not surprising that many groups can adapt it to achieve successful results.

Connecting the Dots

My research went beyond the boundaries of science, psychology, twelve-step programs, and religion to find solutions that effectively solved problems with emotions and relationships. It became apparent that most people who had succeeded in solving serious problems and finding long-term happiness and peace had three distinct life phases in common:

1. They had initially suffered emotional misery.
   (Common problem: deep emotional chaos)
2. They experienced an inner spiritual transformation that altered their attitude and reactions to life.
   (Common answer: an inner spiritual transformation.)
3. Following this transformation, they experienced few of the emotional upsets that previously had disrupted and almost destroyed their lives.
   (Common results: solutions for transcending challenges of living.)

My logical process had worked. It allowed me to find these various groups, recognize the connection among them, and identify a solution!

These people had suffered the same emotional problems that I experienced *and they had found a solution that produced results*. Yet, I hesitated, in spite of this crystal-clear picture. This was not the logical, scientific answer I anticipated. In fact, it seemed diametrically opposed to that. But I couldn't ignore the overwhelming evidence, based on years of unbiased research, that a *spiritual* experience formed the core of this transformation that led to a better life.

I had given up on God and religion years ago. Experience had convinced me that if God existed, he or she delivered no real answers to practical problems. I'd tried different religions. I attended and participated in church, but I still felt anger, fear, worry, and a low sense of self-worth. My prayers did not stop my divorce. I had observed no evidence that anything spiritual worked—until now.

The individuals who had transformed their lives offered a different view of this God-religion-spiritual thing. When I looked for a common thread in their discoveries and methods, I found three points:

1. An inner spiritual transformation formed the basis of these fantastic changes.
2. This innate spiritual essence consisted of a power that supplied a previously un-experienced "energy-for-change," plus it provided a new sense of direction, values, and purpose.
3. This inner spirituality may be found and practiced within, or separate from, organized religion. This personal spiritual relationship is the important element—rather than any particular religion, or lack of religion, or any specific belief.

These distinctions opened my mind a little. The fact that this process centered on an inner power and required no adherence to theological dogma carved a chink in my resistance. These same engineering techniques now guided me in finding a practical concept of spirituality that would provide the power—the raw energy—to achieve this change. These tools helped identify the universal process that had helped other people transform and find lasting happiness, and I began to feel that they could help me.

The Phoenix People

My research revealed a collection of people from all walks of life. They had suffered, undergone a profound inner experience, and emerged to a better way of living. I called this composite group the Phoenix people. They symbolize the story of the beautiful avian creature that would sense its approaching death and burn itself in a cleansing and purifying fire. From the ashes, a new, stronger phoenix would arise.

As I thought about the characteristics of this group, I realized that I have met some of these Phoenix people during my long search for answers. Gene is a wonderful example. A quiet, peaceful man, Gene was totally blind and suffered from crippling arthritis. Born a black man in Southern Oklahoma in the early 1900s, he'd experienced the dark side of life. He had survived the Depression and in later years worked as a sharecropper and laborer. He now lived alone on a minuscule disability income. Despite these adversities, Gene exuded quiet confidence, happiness, and a tranquility of mind that attracted people like a magnet attracts metal. No one who knew Gene ever felt sorry for him.

One day, Gene and I were talking while he was rolling a cigarette. He paused a moment and then said something that has had a deep effect on my entire life. In his gravelly, plainspoken voice, Gene said, "I be a good blind. Lots of folks, they got eyes but they be bad blind. I can see you. I can see God, but they can't. They can't even see other folks. I been blessed."

What a profound way to view adversity!

Gene had the typical attitude and zest for living that Phoenix people demonstrate. They learn to accept and deal with the vicissitudes of life without succumbing to self-pity or melancholy. They discover that pain is inevitable, but misery is optional. With that knowledge, they develop the skills to endure emotional pain but not volunteer for misery.

Emotional pain includes sadness and grief. These feelings are an inevitable part of living. Misery, on the other hand, represents unnecessary negative emotions that detract from the quality of life. Symptoms of misery include unhealthy fear, anger, worry, anxiety, jealousy, envy, self-pity, and resentment. Guilt, shame, disappointment, and feeling betrayed may fall into either category, depending on the source of these emotions. The following chapters have detailed discussions of these feelings as well as guidelines to determine if the individual cases are considered pain or misery. This distinction between emotional pain and misery is critical. The *Spiritual Engineering* process guides us into developing the skills to work through emotional pain and avoid most of the feelings of misery.

Spiritual Engineering Axiom #2

Life gives us pain,
but misery is optional

---

1. Banschjick, Mark. Psychology Today, "The High Failure Rate of Second and Third Marriages." Last modified February 6, 2012. Accessed October 26, 2013. http://www.psychologytoday.com/blog/the-intelligent-divorce/201202/the-high-failure-rate-second-and-third-marriages.
2. divorcerate.org, "divorce rate." Accessed October 26, 2013. http://www.divorcerate.org/
3. "America's #1 Health Problem" Last modified June 29, 2012. Accessed October 26, 2013 http://www.stress.org/americas-1-health-problem/
4. National Institute of Mental Health, "Health and Education." Accessed October 26, 2013. http://www.nimh.nih.gov/statistics/index.shtml.
5. National Institute on Drug Abuse, "The Science of Drug Abuse and Addiction." Accessed October 26, 2013. http://www.drugabuse.gov/drugs-abuse
6. Center for Disease Control and Prevention, "Overweight and Obesity." Accessed October 26, 2013. http://www.cdc.gov/obesity/data/index.html.
7. James, William. *Varieties of Religious Experience*. Random House, 1994.

8. Maslow, Abraham. *Religions, Values, and Peak Experiences.* New York: Penguin Compass, 1979.
9. Maslow, Abraham. *Toward a Psychology of Being.* New York: John Wiley and Sons, 1999.

The Natural Order: The Principles of Spiritual Engineering

"Science without religion is lame; Religion without science is blind."

—Albert Einstein

When I began my quest for answers, I discovered that I held a huge resentment against two people over an incident from years past. I still felt that they had wronged me. Every time I thought of them, or the event, I felt anger, a sense of unfairness and helplessness well up inside me. I would have enjoyed making life unbearable for them.

Clyde, a friend I admired, asked me, "Tom, do you enjoy feeling this way? This situation that upsets you so much happened a long time ago. The two people involved have moved on with their lives. They probably don't even think about what happened. But just the thought of them has the power to make you upset. Do you realize that you give these people power over you? You still allow them to dictate your feelings like you are a puppet on a string."

Of course, I didn't want them controlling anything about me, and I didn't like feeling this upset. Then he told me he had learned a prayer in AA that helped him with resentments. If I wanted to get rid of this resentment, he said I should pray for these people for thirty days, asking God to give them everything I valued and wanted in life—love, peace of mind, and happiness. I thought that was ridiculous.

I said, "Clyde, you're crazy. I hate these people. I want to hurt them, not help them. I'd be lying if I asked God to help them."

He responded quietly, "Tom, just tell God the truth about how you feel and try this."

I distinctly remember getting down on my knees, feeling foolish and a little afraid, saying,

> God, I don't believe that this will work and I'm not very sure about you either. I really don't want you to do this, but I've been told that this will make me feel better. I really hate Jane and Mike for what they did and I'd like to see them suffer; but every time I think of them it tears me up inside, and I want to quit hurting.
>
> So if you're out there, I ask you, please give them love, peace of mind, health, and happiness. Help them find a wonderful life.
>
> Now, God, I'll tell you again that I really don't mean this and I don't want you to do it.

The first couple of times I said this, I paused at the end, waiting expectantly, and somewhat fearfully. When I realized that I didn't get zapped by lightning for talking to God that way, the fear started melting away. After two weeks, I noticed that I was skipping the part about not meaning it and not wanting God to do it. After a month, I could actually think of what had happened without being pulled down by the misery. This was the first time I had ever told God the truth about my less-than-heavenly feelings, the first time I had really been honest in my spiritual relationship. And the results were unbelievable. I could remember the experience of what had happened without having feelings attached to it; the anger, bitterness, and hatred were completely gone.

This was another turning point in my quest. I had entered this experiment being very skeptical about God and whether praying ever got results. My recurring misery made me willing to follow instructions from someone who had what I wanted—peace of mind and happiness. I emerged with new understandings based on the *actual changes in my life*. I had no measurable external scientific facts, but the transformation in my inner life was real and valid. As an engineer, I look for process, action, and results. This was the real thing. It produced results.

Basis of the Process

Over the last two centuries, science and engineering have achieved great advances for humanity. Science discovers, tests, and formulates laws that describe the material world. Engineering applies these scientific principles in order to change and improve this physical reality. An engineering analysis revealed similar backgrounds, similar processes, and dramatic improvements in the lives of the Phoenix people. These same techniques also generated a step-by-step process that any willing person can use to enjoy the awesome life these people experience. Applying engineering logic to the spiritual quest helps us access and unleash the energy of transformation. The term *Spiritual Engineering* describes this unique integration of science and spirituality.

Don't worry if you don't have a scientific or engineering bone in your body. This doesn't require a bit of math! Let's take a quick look at a scientific law that will demonstrate how the rules that affect our natural world also apply remarkably well to our feelings and relationships. Let's start with a natural law that may not be well known, but you will soon recognize its impact on your life.

Why Your House Gets Dirty and
Your Relationships Deteriorate

The Second Law of Thermodynamics describes *entropy*—an interesting physical law that says nature tends to move things from order to disorder, from stability to instability. This may sound a little complicated at first, but it's really not. Everything naturally deteriorates, if left alone and work—expending energy—is the only thing that can prevent this decline.

This principle applies to many areas in your life. You can spend hours cleaning your house, and it reverts to disorder and chaos before your very eyes—or at least within a few days. Forget to pay attention to what you eat and watch what happens to your weight and your waistline. Leave a piece of iron exposed to the elements and it will soon weaken and discolor with rust. These examples demonstrate the inexorable effects of entropy.

This universal law affects our feelings and relationships as surely as it does our physical world. Without work, any relationship will deteriorate. Even the most vibrant, passionate association cannot withstand the deteriorating pull of entropy, if we don't spend energy on its maintenance and upkeep. Anger, worry, jealousy, blame, and so on are often the rust and dust symptoms of a relationship that is succumbing to entropy.

Okay, this makes sense. We know we must work but it also helps if we understand some things about energy so our efforts get the desired results.

Personal Energy and Natural Laws

This process expands our awareness of personal energy—how we get it, how it affects our lives, and how we can get the best results from what energy we have. Let's start with some basic ideas about physical energy and see how that can apply to our other personal energies.

Let's look at the law of the conservation of energy. Again, this may sound a little complicated but it's really very simple when we apply it to our personal energy. On this level, it says that an individual only has a specific quantity of energy available that can be used to accomplish work. When we use it, it's gone and we must replenish the energy before doing more work. We work, we get tired, and we rest to replenish our energy. To overcome this limitation, humanity has learned to use external sources of physical energy. Electricity, hydrocarbon fuel, and solar power are a few examples of these energies that significantly advance our quality of life. Just imagine what life would be like without them. What if we could find and use similar types of energy that would drastically improve our inner life and relationships? Well, that is exactly what we're going to do.

Spiritual Engineering offers techniques to 1) tap into additional energy sources in our non-physical levels and 2) to improve our inner-energy efficiency so that we see more results for less effort.

We can summarize these points in a few straightforward statements:

1. If left alone, many aspects of our lives will deteriorate into disorder and chaos (entropy).
2. Work is required to overcome the deteriorating effect of entropy.
3. We only have a set amount of personal energy available to do the work, so we use additional sources of power to augment our personal energies.
4. Working at higher efficiency and effectiveness lets us accomplish more with our accessible energy.

We accept how this works on the physical level. Now we can apply these and similar concepts to emotions and relationships which will remove some of the mystery from these important parts of our lives.

Relationships and Stinky Air

Our feelings—both the painful and wonderful ones—start and grow in relationships. That's it. Bottom line. Our emotions, self-esteem, social acceptance, fulfillment, and gratification revolve around these personal interactions.

Our high divorce rates indicate that we have serious underlying problems with relationships. Our best attempts fail at an alarming frequency. Many of us don't understand what constitutes a healthy relationship, how to form successful relationships, or when or how to sever unhealthy relationships. We often accept mediocrity and misery as normal. This current relationship paradigm makes our chances of experiencing a fantastic relationship a matter of luck.

Paradigms like this are dangerous. They can destroy lives. The old miasma theory is a good example. Nineteenth century physicians used the miasma theory to explain the spread of sickness such as cholera, diphtheria, and smallpox. This concept postulated that bad-smelling air, known as miasma, caused these deadly diseases. The physicians and scientists of that age observed that these diseases became rampant when the air started smelling really bad. Of course, raw sewage and poor sanitation were the true source of the stinky air. At times, the disgusting odor would become overpowering and the leaders would initiate programs to overcome the stench. They would clean up the sewage and this would result in some sporadic health improvements. Of course, miasma proponents said that these improvements validated their theory—the outbreak of disease decreased when they got rid of the stinky air.

The basic assumption, although completely wrong, did produce some positive, short-term results because of the work directed to relieve the symptoms; however, little hope for a true solution existed while people accepted the flawed paradigm.

Louis Pasteur introduced his germ theory in 1875. He fought an uphill battle, trying to convince the medical profession that their unsanitary practices spread germs that killed patients. The doctors would not concede that something invisible to the best scientific methods of the time could cause fatal illness. They derided and belittled Pasteur. Well-intentioned physicians continued to cause death because they would not change their beliefs. Like a chick that's pecking and cracking its eggshell, Pasteur's new concept had to break out of the existing paradigm to birth a new and effective answer.

The current dismal state of relationships in our lives reflects a similar situation. Some people do experience sporadic and temporary success, which appears to validate the current theory; advocates tout that these intermittent improvements prove that their method is correct. However, an objective overview reveals that our approach is a dismal failure. We can rationalize and find excuses, but nothing can disprove the cold, hard fact that hundreds of millions still suffer. As in the past, many scientists persist in discounting any force that cannot be measured with current instruments.

Sounds a little like the miasma theory, doesn't it? If we want better relationships, we simply have to break this existing paradigm and find a new way to solve the problems. The concept of a natural order provides the key.

A Natural Order

There's a hard way and there's an easy way to do many things in life. We use terms like "on the beam, in the groove, and going with the flow" to describe these. For example, canoeing downstream requires much less work than going upstream. Even people who have never paddled a canoe accept that going *against* the current requires much more energy than going *with* the current. The river's energy can either help us along or retard our progress. Going with the flow requires effort; going against it, struggle.

Going with the flow represents the easiest way to go canoeing or to move along the stream of life. This represents a natural order in the physical world—a way that helps us accomplish more by aligning our energy with a natural, pre-existent energy to help achieve our objective. *Harmonizing our efforts with natural laws simply works better than going against them.*

Once again, we can apply this principle from nature to relationships to help us understand and achieve our objectives. The Phoenix People exemplify this technique. They have ceased struggling by applying this principle of a natural order to build relationships that absolutely transform their lives.

The Natural Order of Relationships

At one point in my life I decided to build a house. I hadn't done anything like that before, but I thought I could do it if I developed a good process before I started. I researched house construction, talked with contractors, bought blueprints, and prepared a detailed procedure to follow. I reviewed it with contractors who were currently building nice homes. I completed all this before I moved the first shovel of dirt. I went back to the experienced people for direction a few times, but I managed to end up with a nice house.

However, for some unfathomable reason, I thought I could just go out and have great relationships because that's what I wanted to happen. It didn't work that way. I found that wonderful relationships, like houses, have to be built—they don't just happen. The best relationships also follow natural laws. They contain the proper components and are constructed in a well-defined order.

Spiritual Engineering Axiom #3

Extraordinary relationships are built;
they don't just happen

The pieces needed to build extraordinary relationships turned out to be simple, but they were definitely not what I had expected. All my life, when I thought of relationships, I always considered they were associations with other people. Soon I discovered that associations with other people are just one category of relationships. There are actually three possible types of relationships. The Natural Order for Relationships consists of having: 1) a primary relationship with our personal inner spiritual essence, 2) a relationship with our self, and 3) relationships with other people. This order is extremely important. Believing that human-to-human interaction forms the totality of our relationships contributes to our current flawed paradigm. This eliminates the possibility of following the natural order and automatically dooms us to failure or second-rate personal associations.

Recognizing these distinct types of relationships is the first step, but how do we assemble these to produce the highest-quality relationships? Building relationships this way has some similarities to building a house. In both cases, we need to begin by building a foundation, then we erect the walls—the supporting structure—and lastly, we add the roof.

In building effective relationships, a spiritual relationship, one that establishes our values, purpose, and direction for life, forms the foundation; our relationship with self constitutes the walls; and relationships with other people become the roof. A joyful and vibrant life requires building and nurturing all three types of relationships and maintaining this prioritized order. No other model for relationships follows the natural order, and alternative methods inevitably result in struggle, chaos, and misery. Constructing relationships this way dramatically improves success in all relationships.

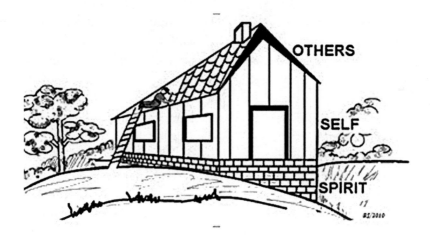

If we're building a house, we wouldn't consider working on the roof before the walls and underpinning were solid; however, we repeatedly do this with relationships, and then we wonder why they come crashing down. We focus our attention and effort on our relationship with the other person while we ignore a crumbling foundation and the cracks in the supporting structure.

Spiritual Engineering Axiom #4

The Natural Order for Relationships is:

1. A relationship with our inner spirit
2. A relationship with self
3. Relationships with others

The Spiritual Relationship: The Foundation

By now you realize that I changed from being a pragmatic, almost agnostic, engineer into accepting a spiritual relationship as the foundation of all my relationships. This dramatic change was not instantaneous or easily accepted. My extensive research, along with discussions with hundreds of people, persuaded me that this spiritual transformation might be valid. I could see the results of it in those who had enjoyed this experience. They had found a way to avoid the miseries of life that haunted me; they had built the quality of relationships I wanted.

But I faced a dilemma. I had long ago given up on the idea that God or any super-natural force interceded in individual lives. I had repeatedly tried to use my willpower and my intelligence to solve my emotional and relationship problems. My emotional turmoil, near-suicide, alcoholism, and lack of healthy relationships highlighted the abject failure of these methods. I may be stubborn, but I got tired of hurting. Repeatable, confirmable results finally convinced me of the existence of a spiritual force; the same way the physicians of the nineteenth century finally became convinced that Pasteur's germ theory was valid. However, I was still not prepared to accept any belief or faith—I needed a pragmatic spirituality.

Spiritual Engineering focuses on the process—taking action and getting results. It differs from some organized approaches to spirituality because it asks you to take the guided action, experience the results, and then define your personal belief based on these results. It's not important whether you believe in God, have rejected religion and God, have any spiritual faith, or even believe that this is a bunch of "touchy-feely mumbo-jumbo." If you want to experience freedom from emotional misery, be open to the *possibility* that this spiritual transformation *might* be possible, that there might be chance that a power exists inside of you that can change your life. Then you can try the process and base your conclusions on the results you experience in your own life.

I later realized that spirituality adds another dimension to life. It adds a third dimension, a depth, to the mental and the physical (material) parts. This dimension offers each of us an opportunity to access values, direction, purpose, and principles—those nonphysical and extra-mental assets that contribute greatly to our quality of life.

I researched different religions, psychology, and science, and observed what worked and did not work for other people trying this path. I'll share a few conclusions from this search for God and spirituality with the caveat that these work for me and have worked for many other people, but everyone must find his or her own personal concepts. I offer these as a starting point. Agree or disagree with the ideas I present, but let them stimulate you into a search for your own concepts.

A Self-Relationship: The Supporting Structure

We spend more time in the self-relationship than any other because we live with ourselves 24/7. We are in the middle of every interaction, every thought, and every feeling. We mentally ask our self, "What should I do in this situation?" or "What if this happens?" or "Why did he or she do that?" and on and on. This internal process evaluates events, judges their impact on us, and makes decisions. It forms the eyes through which we see the world. When this self-relationship is out of balance, it distorts our view of everything.

Have you ever seen mirrors in a funhouse that make you look taller, shorter, skinnier, or fatter? An unhealthy self-relationship skews your perception as surely as these mirrors, distorting your view of yourself and other people. These deformed images can convince you that you really are "less than" or "better than" and influence your outlook on everything.

This relationship forms the womb for all anger, guilt, anxiety, low self-esteem, fear, worry, shame, jealousy, and every other feeling of misery. Experiencing some of life's events and loving other people may cause emotional pain at times, but misery is self-inflicted and a direct result of an unhealthy self-relationship. Lack of integrity and the absence of an effective decision-making process form the core of problems in this area. The word *integrity* springs from the root word *integer*—the quality or condition of being whole, complete, undivided, and unimpaired. Lacking wholeness leaves a hole. We are either complete or we're incomplete. We are either whole or have a hole. The current emotional chaos and relationship failures in our world demonstrate the results of filling this void with chemicals, possessions, or immature relationships. However, using this logical process will give us a chance to fill this hole with something that will restore our integrity and bring us back into the natural order.

Relationships with Others: The Roof—The Crowning Achievement

With an initial foundation and some supporting structure in place, there are only two rules we have to follow to experience exceptional relationships:

- Be loving.
- Love with wisdom.

Unfortunately, our current relationship paradigm does not teach us how to do either of these, but don't be discouraged, these are learnable skills. Anyone can enjoy them when the paradigm is broken and the natural order is followed.

Love is simply an active, healthy concern for someone's well-being. That's all it is. Nothing fancy or mysterious, but it applies to every relationship we will ever have. The *active* and *healthy* descriptors are extremely important. Love flows from what we do, not from what we say. Building love on a foundation of integrity and applying it with wisdom follows the natural way and yields the maximum benefits. Phoenix People bestow and receive love with the wisdom and ease that come from following these universal principles. In fact, they share many similar attributes in all three of the primal relationships.

In the spiritual relationship, Phoenix People:

- recognize the existence of a spiritual aspect to life, though they may perceive and define it very differently from other people
- have tremendous tolerance for other spiritual beliefs
- believe in the overall friendliness of the universe (demonstrate a positive outlook on life)
- have faith, *based on results*, that this spiritual power can relieve emotional misery.

In the self-relationship, they:

- strive for physical, mental, and spiritual integration
- differentiate between pain and misery, and seldom suffer great depths or frequencies of misery
- approach living challenges as opportunities for growth
- demonstrate a gentle sense of humor
- live in the present moment. They:
  - remember the experience of negative past events to avoid repeating mistakes but have no emotional reactions associated with those events
  - exist relatively free of worry or anxiety.

In relationships with other people, they:

- display genuine interest in all human beings, evidenced by their desire for loving service
- form relationships to augment, but not create, their happiness, fulfillment, and joy;
- do not allow other people to unduly influence or create their feelings
- love with wisdom.

The Proof: Results

Following efficient methods of doing things (though they may sound like nothing more than common sense) leads to the zenith of human development. Remember, natural orders just *are*—they do not require our approval any more than a river current needs our opinion on which direction it should flow. We have to discern the flow and choose to travel with that flow.

Can these methods work to solve our life's challenges? Can learning to apply scientific and engineering principles to emotions and relationships really improve our quality of life?

Living this way, following these principles, has seen me through the deaths of my mother, of brothers and sisters, my dearly loved nineteen-year-old stepdaughter, and my wife of twenty-one years. It yielded serenity and lack of fear when I lost the vision in both of my eyes and specialists did not expect me to ever see again. On a daily basis, it gives me practical solutions to everyday challenges—how to deal with difficult situations at work; how to deal with people who try to manipulate and control; and how to enjoy life in the midst of turmoil. It has melted the worry, low self-worth, fear, and anxiety that plagued my life. These are typical results, experienced by many who have tried this process.

This is not about simply surviving difficult times, or merely coping with problems and challenges. It's far more than that. These systematic methods produce a life-altering transformation that moves people from turmoil to serenity, from tragedy to triumph, from misery to happiness, and from mediocrity to extraordinary success in their relationships. These techniques synthesize science, spirituality, and commonsense psychology to define the three primal relationships of life and their inter-connectedness. Then, this logical, systematic approach identifies, for each of these relationships: 1) the problem, 2) the solution, and 3) the most effective way to implement this solution to transform your life

Each of us has a birthright to happiness; however, actually experiencing it requires that we take certain actions. Every time we say or think, "I could be happy if..," we choose to delay this wonderful gift. Happiness is a *now* event—not tomorrow's promise.

It all starts with building a solid foundation.

PART TWO

A Spiritual Relationship: The Foundation for All Relationships

Developing a Spiritual Relationship: The Problem

"Creeds grow so thick along the way their boughs hide God."

—Lizette Woodworth Reese

The cold Wyoming wind sapped the strength from our subdued search party. Flashlights pierced the oncoming darkness and highlighted the heavy snow that continued to fall. If we couldn't find him soon, this would be the second night that Billy had spent exposed to the subzero weather. Hope faded with the decreasing daylight. Many of us tried to find comfort in the thought that the nineteen-year-old had grown up in this kind of severe weather.

Billy had left his friends to cross-country ski back to the car alone. They waited for hours but he never arrived. Search and rescue started at daylight but the previous night's snow had obliterated all tracks. Family, friends, and the entire community held a candlelight vigil at his mother's church. They prayed and implored God for Billy's safe return. They had faith that God would answer their prayers. But they were wrong. We found Billy under a foot of snow. The prayers did not stop the hyperthermia.

Disappointed Believers and Skeptics

Such a death wrenches the heart and soul of parents, family, and friends. But what Billy's parents, Bob and Elaine, found in that church compounded their grief. Instead of finding comfort and solace, they heard that God had taken their son, that He must need Billy for some purpose, that they should not question the ways of the Lord, and that perhaps God had chosen not to grant the petitions for his safety because of a lack of faith.

Elaine and Bob rejected the church after hearing this. They said they wanted no part of a God who would whimsically take their son or promise to answer their prayers and then ignore them in the time of their greatest need. Feelings of betrayal, guilt, and isolation added to their deep mourning.

On June 5, 1968, more than twenty years before Billy's parents faced this ordeal, U.S. Senator and presidential hopeful Robert Kennedy was shot in the Ambassador Hotel in Los Angeles. He laid in a hospital overnight, his fate unknown. I watched as thousands of clergy and millions of believers around the world prayed for his life. I visualized a large stream of prayer emanating like a cloud from the earth to the heavens and God. I remember specifically thinking that if prayer does get God to intercede—to change the course of human events—this would be the time. God could not ignore this unified petition from so many faithful believers, which included some of the greatest religious leaders on the planet.

Bobby Kennedy died twenty-five hours later.

This event and lack of divine response validated my beliefs that supernatural forces may exist but they do nothing to help us work out our problems in this world. I was convinced that hard work and determination got better results than any belief in prayer, or faith in an unseen God. Logical science appeared to produce more reliable results.

Yet, in the years between this assassination and Billy's death, I completely reversed this conclusion. Thankfully, by then I could share with Elaine and Bob that God had not failed them or Billy. I was able to offer explanations based on different concepts that they found acceptable. The logical approach to spirituality worked for them. As it had for me, it opened the door for a wonderful relationship with their personal inner divine presence and taught them how to receive results from prayer.

When it comes to God, in this modern age, many people are like Billy's parents—disappointed believers and skeptics. We accept science because it produces results. Along with millions like us, there are the Sunday-go-to-church-but-forget-it-during-the-week believers, agnostics, and atheists. Many find it difficult to overcome the barriers between logic and belief, between science and faith.

Modern Roadblocks to Faith

Make no mistake—a lot of people still believe in God. However, many do not consider religion or spirituality important to their daily living experiences. Some have firmly rejected the idea of God or anything that cannot be proven by science; others simply believe that these concepts have little bearing in a modern world. People give numerous reasons for these negative or neutral views about spirituality; some of the more common ones include:

1. Science. Science produces results; this God idea doesn't. If I can't see it or touch it, or if it can't be proven by science, then, it's not real and has no substance.
2. Materialism. I live in a material world. I have a mortgage, medical bills, and kids going to college. God won't help pay my bills or do anything about the real problems I have.
3. Self-driven attitudes. A myriad of *self-driven* mind-sets prevents the open-mindedness necessary for investigation. A few of these are:
   o Self-sufficiency: I don't need God or religion—I know that determination, intelligence, and effort are the keys to a successful life.
   o Self-centeredness: It's all about me; I have to take care of number one.
   o Selfishness: I believe I deserve more than other people.
   o Self-gratification: If it feels good, do it. Take it, buy it, swallow it, or get it any way you can.
   o Self-righteousness: What I believe, think, or do is right. Other people have a right to their opinions, but I don't need to seriously consider them because I already know the answers.
4. Misconceptions. Erroneous beliefs about this spiritual life deter, or actually offend, the logical thinker. The disharmony and sometimes out-right animosity among

organized religions contribute to this. Below are just a few common arguments people present:

- Religions argue about God. Christianity can't even agree on the details of their Bible or on important concepts.
- Religion does not work. I've tried it; going to church didn't do anything for me.
- If God exists, why would anyone want anything to do with a God that causes earthquakes, genocide, and famines, or a God that takes people we love away and allows events like 9/11 to happen?
- Science has proven that evolution is a fact, but many religions want to deny this or twist it to fit their preconceived beliefs. If they are wrong about this, they could be wrong about God.
- Why do I need God? I'm doing okay. Religion is for the weak, those who can't make it in the world on their own.

5. Deiphobia. In addition to these more obvious obstacles to spirituality, a fear that is best described as deiphobia pervades modern humanity. This is not a fear *of* God; it *is* the fear of allowing God, or any spiritual concept, to actively participate in all aspects of daily life—the fear of exchanging a self-driven will for some nebulous spiritual principle. People are afraid that personal spirituality may limit their freedom, their fun, and their self-identity. Their comments follow along these lines:

- I don't want a righteous life that's dull and boring.
- I don't want God watching over my shoulder all the time. I want to enjoy myself and have fun.
- Besides, if I let God run my life, what will happen to me? Will I be like the hole in the doughnut—like my willpower, intelligence, and desires count for nothing?

These widespread ideas raise valid concerns. Any answers that are clear and powerful enough to overcome these doubts must have a logical basis and offer evidence that can withstand unbiased evaluations.

I subscribed to many of those reasons. But the results of my research, coupled with a deep desire to find real solutions, drove me to be open-minded enough to experiment with new concepts. Still, I needed something more than people telling me that I just had to "Have faith" or "Our way is the only way—believe or perish." I needed intellectually defensible concepts that felt consistent and didn't force me to choose between God and science or between belief and logic.

Developing a Spiritual Relationship: The Solution

"I do not feel obliged to believe that the same God who has endowed us with sense, reason, and intellect has intended us to forgo their use."

—C.S Lewis

I didn't seek a spiritual path because I wanted to be good or be saved—I just wanted to be happy. Despite my bias, I became convinced that personal spirituality would play a key role. In the past, I had blithely relegated the God idea to weaker, less intellectual people, but I had to reassess my conclusions. I had to find concepts that fit the world I observed, that eradicated my barriers to spirituality. I needed something that went beyond the rhetoric of religionists I had heard trying to explain why God allowed natural disasters, wars, child abuse, genocide, and so on, and that delivered *verifiable and repeatable results* to solve the problems of living. After all, if God didn't help with real problems, I wasn't sure I needed Him.

God and Groucho

Before looking at these ideas, let's discuss the word *God*. Don't get hung up on this. It's just a word used to describe a universally recognized concept. Feel free to substitute Allah, Universal Spirit,

Buddha, Great Spirit, Divine Mother, the Tao, Supreme Being, Higher Power, or whatever you like. My friend Carla called it Groucho when she started this spiritual journey.

In her early teens, Carla had been forced into prostitution, and she had succumbed to drug addiction and alcoholism. She wanted nothing to do with God; in fact, she thought that if he existed at all, he certainly had done nothing to help her. When she started her recovery, she heard that this Higher Power would help her break the addiction and give her a chance to be happy and free. Despite her initial resistance, Carla finally accepted that she needed some kind of a spiritual life, but she still rejected the word *God*.

The only enjoyable moments she could remember and the one interruption from her daily misery and degradation was when she was able to watch the comedian Groucho Marx on television. He made her laugh for a few minutes. This single pleasant memory became the starting point for her new life. If this Higher Power could help her enjoy life, he might be a little like the comedian. He might be fun to get to know. For two years, she called her God, Groucho.

From this beginning, Carla forged a rewarding spiritual relationship that she now considers the cornerstone of her new life. Hope, optimism, and self-confidence replaced fear, resentments, anxiety, and anger. She got a GED and a college degree, and then she dedicated her life to work for children's rights. Carla said that her worst experiences helped her bridge the painful emotional gap and interact with an abused child. Typical of the Phoenix People's response, instead of allowing her adversities to defeat her, she used them as the impetus to great accomplishments.

Unlike Carla, I didn't have a problem with the word *God*, but I needed concepts that would fit with my logical approach to life. I had discovered that my expectations about people were often the cause of my turmoil. I would expect a person to act in a certain way, and when he or she failed to live up to my expectation, I would feel angry, disappointed, hurt, or rejected. Eventually, I realized that my preconceived ideas about God and religion were having exactly the same effect. If I expected responses that were not likely to happen, I would get disappointed or even feel betrayed by God. I had to find a way to build healthy expectations about this spiritual power, expectations that were consistent with facts and results. I had witnessed extraordinary manifestations in people's lives that seemed connected to this spiritual power. I knew that this power— the driving energy for the transformation—existed, but I had to align my expectations with something that would work. I had to open up to and explore different ideas about God because what I had been taught in the past didn't yield the results I needed.

Search and Research

I spent years in an extensive research effort. I read books ranging from the *Bible*, the *Koran*, the *Upanishads*, the *Bhagavad Gita*, the *Tao Te Ching*, the *Book of Mormon*, the *Urantia Book*, *A Course in Miracles*, *Black Elk Speaks*, and writings on prayer and meditation, to the works of Carl Jung and psychologists William James, Abraham Maslow, Albert Ellis, and others. I sought out people who had enjoyed a spiritual transformation or peak experiences, and I earned a master's degree in psychology. I attended powwows, medicine wheel ceremonies, and spirit quests of Native Americans. I lived in the Sultanate of Oman, where I made close Muslim friends and was honored to spend time in their homes. I visited Buddhist temples in Thailand, and I witnessed the residual legacy of the Tao, from Beijing to rural China.

Whether I was talking with a practicing religionist, a PhD psychologist, or a recovering alcoholic, I looked for *observable results* in their lives. What were the verifiable consequences? I also looked for a step-by-step procedure. These ideas of God, faith, and spirituality seemed amorphous, and I wanted to distill them into a process I could follow.

In this chapter and the next, I'll present some practical concepts I gleaned from this research. If you like them, that's great. If not, allow them to stimulate you into finding what works for you. This is not about believing what I believe or blindly accepting any theology. Find the path that works for you. Our personal concept of how we view God and what he or she does or does not do is extremely important. It forms the foundation of our expectations about spirituality and helps clarify what we see as our role in this divine/human relationship.

The *Spiritual Engineering* approach offers benefits for a variety of personal belief systems.

- Approaching this connection with a spiritual being as an actual *relationship* offers advantages, including a wide range of options. Accepting God as a loving, spiritual parent, the ancestor of the spiritual force, and a guiding inner compass opens us to the maximum relationship potential. Anyone having trouble accepting the divine-parent approach might retain the relationship concept by seeing this entity as a spiritual friend and guide. This still suggests the potential of a loving, personal entity who cares for each one of us, who wants the best for us, and who will extend help, direction, care, and comfort whenever we need it.
- For those who see God as energy or presence, these techniques offer a method to increase the flow of that energy and allow it to work more effectively in their lives.
- Those who hold a steadfast belief that the mind is the key to happiness will find pragmatic methods to remove mental clutter and focus their intellectual energy.
- For those who do not believe in spiritual matters at all, this process offers practical guidelines for solving the challenges of daily life that yield dramatic and precise benefits.

These plain, straightforward methods are universal. They simply work.

The Primal Relationship

Among the myriad ideas about the God-human connection, *Spiritual Engineering* presents this interaction as a relationship. This premise opens the door to other spiritual concepts to be discussed in this section. This does not minimize the energy aspect of an inner divine spark; it only suggests that it possesses attributes in addition to energy. God offers every one of us the opportunity for this personal relationship. Each of us must use our power of choice and decide whether to participate or not.

I was pretty skeptical at the beginning, so I tried to find a way to reconcile this relationship idea with what I observed. I realized that I could accept God as a spiritual parent and all the people on this planet as God's spiritual children. Growing up without a father caused me some initial problems with this concept, but it also gave me a chance to develop my own ideas about the perfect father–child relationship. I discovered that it makes little difference whether you see this deity as having masculine, feminine, or combined attributes. For simplicity, I'll use masculine pronouns, but feel free to substitute whatever fits your image of this divine being.

God, as the perfect parent, loves each of us with infinite love, patience, and tolerance, along with a perfect balance of mercy, compassion, and justice. To him, we are young immature children. He knows we'll make mistakes and that we will develop and grow with experience. No matter our age or seeming maturity, we truly are *children* of the eternal divine being—not adult offspring of some Higher Power.

I came to see that this path of spiritual growth will take a long time and that, to some degree, I will remain a spiritual child all my life. I think God may see us as I viewed my children when they were about two years old. I didn't expect them to act like adults with wisdom and maturity or to know how to do everything. I fully expected them to be children and to act like children. When they'd stumble and fall, get frustrated and cry, or need a loving hug, I'd try to help them—if they would accept my help. The important thing for me as a parent was that they were making progress, albeit sometimes slowly.

This concept provides an alternative view to the idea that we need to both love and fear God—that He is simultaneously wrathful, vengeful, jealous, and angry, as well as loving, compassionate, merciful, and just. We can view such seeming contradictions as that of a child coming to know his or her parent. As a child matures in a caring family, love increasingly replaces fear. The *God as spiritual parent* idea leads to other interesting correlations. Our physical father contributes genetic material that influences some of our attributes, such as intellect, height, and the color of our hair and eyes. Likewise, our spiritual father provides the seed for the spiritual part of us. We receive a spiritual DNA that responds to spiritual gravity like our physical body responds to physical gravity. It yields an inner magnetic pull that tugs us toward the spirit. In addition to this direct inheritance, we receive two gifts that are part of our marvelous birthright.

The first gift represents the most powerful asset in our life—the power of free will. We've been given the power to choose our responses to life—we choose our attitude, we choose misery or happiness, and we choose our ultimate destiny. Only natural laws limit this power. We cannot simply choose to defy gravity or go back in time to change something that already happened. Nonetheless, we do have tremendous latitude in how we act and react in our life's situations.

We can choose whether we engage in or reject this spiritual relationship, and we can choose how actively we allow God to participate in our lives. Just as they do in the physical realm, decisions involving our spiritual life also carry consequences. But in the spiritual domain, the consequences may not be immediately obvious. For example, God doesn't directly punish us if we reject the spiritual life, but that decision limits the resources that are available to help us solve our problems. Rejecting this removes us from the natural order. This deprives us not only of our primal spiritual relationship but of its accompanying spiritual energy as well—the two key ingredients necessary for achieving maximum benefit from this life. Then, we will find our self more prone to anger, worry, stress, or other miseries, and failed relationships. We seldom realize we have made choices that relinquish the very energy and support that would prevent this suffering.

The second gift is also fantastic. God gives us a divine spark that lives within us. This *kingdom of heaven within* is a direct and personal connection to our divine parent. When we decide to seek a spiritual path, this inner beacon guides our steps. It provides the energy needed for the journey, and it also powers the transformation that can dramatically improve our quality of life. This God fragment is always subservient to our free will; it only helps us make changes in our life *after we choose to do so*. It's only a *potential* power until we make the decision and take the action that allows it to participate.

This concept of potential power is important. We see it all the time in the physical world, but it also applies to our inner spiritual energy. It describes a form of energy that requires something to activate it, to change it into a recognizable, usable force. A physical example of this would be your car's battery. It contains potential power that goes completely unnoticed until you turn the ignition switch. You make a decision and then take an action to consummate that decision. Both parts—the decision *and* the action—are necessary to utilize the potential energy source. The energy-in-waiting then transforms into a real energy that produces very specific and concrete results.

A similar decision/action sequence is what activates the potential spiritual power that resides within each one of us.

Science and Spirituality

As I struggled with merging science and spirituality together in my life, it helped me to remember the story of the blind men who described an elephant after touching different parts of it. Each of them steadfastly swore that his partial perception was the correct description of the elephant. And so it was—of that one piece of reality. Science and spirituality see different views of the one total reality, but they never need to be foes. If they continue progressing, each may see the entire elephant. Science deals with the material aspects of life—physical measurements, facts, and quantity; spirituality concerns deal with the nonphysical side— ideals, the inner life, and our attitude.

Science has made such great material accomplishments that some of us consider it nearly infallible in many realms. However, credible scientific assessment applies *only* to physical reality. That's all it will ever accurately measure. It cannot measure nonphysical reality. For example, no scientific apparatus will ever accurately measure a mother's love for her child. Scientific instruments can measure heartbeat, breath, and perspiration; they can detect and quantify chemicals released by the body when close to, or thinking about, the object of love. They can even differentiate shifts in brain waves that are associated with these thoughts, and on and on. But these are the physical responses to love and *not* the underlying reality. Some part of love exists beyond these components.

In the same way, science can measure the physical aspects of God (all parts of material creation), but some spiritual part exists outside this purely physical realm. Science can never measure that part or prove the existence of such non-material reality. However, the scientific process can help evaluate and compare the effectiveness of practical spirituality. *If we accept results as proof, we can quantify dramatic life improvements in this results-oriented approach.* If an investigator is open-minded enough to actually try this results-oriented method, he or she can experience the proof, the living results.

Religion and Spirituality

Many people fail to benefit from a spiritual life because they are indifferent or antagonistic toward organized religion. Others think that attending church automatically yields spiritual benefits. Both groups may miss the exhilarating experience of finding solutions for living problems because they fail to distinguish between religion and spirituality.

Spirituality refers to the relationship, the personal interaction, between the individual, and his or her concept of God. This relationship is as real as the one between a husband and wife. It's not a one-day-a-week event—it requires 24/7 participation. It stands as the foundation of all relationships. No one stands between an individual and God. Spirituality can be practiced within, or separate from organized religion.

Effective spiritual living produces tangible results in real-life situations. It's not an abstract idea; it actually delivers specific consequences *now* for the actions taken *now*. Connecting with this inner energy supplies the power to change habits and behaviors that are difficult or impossible to change with determination and self-will alone. This spiritual energy guides us in transcending the inevitable pains of life while it progressively offers guidance and power to minimize debilitating misery.

Developing a personal relationship with this internal spiritual entity requires courage and persistence. True spirituality accesses the power to produce a life transformation, a way of living that is beyond the mundane existence experienced by so many people, and a peace that is beyond human understanding. It leaves us forever free to follow the truth, wherever the leadings of our inner spirit may guide us.

God and Evil

I used to wonder why God allowed evil to exist. Why does he let some people do horrendous things to others? If he loves us, why does he allow devastating wars and genocide?

Let's define evil as an act that goes against the principles of good in the universe, or if you wish against God's will. This can range from an action that affects an individual to actions that bring pain and suffering to millions. The act of committing such a deed started right when someone made the choice to consummate the evil act, rather than choosing a different action or choosing to do nothing. This connection between evil and freewill choice can help us see a different view of this God-and-evil dichotomy.

God doesn't create evil. The *potential* for evil is inherent in our ability to make decisions. Here again appears the idea of something existing in potential and only becoming real as a result of someone's choice or action. Having a choice means that we'll have opportunities to choose between right and wrong. For example, we may have to decide between telling the truth or a lie. The choice is in the decision point, the Y in the road. Telling the lie only exists *in potential* until we consummate it. It does not really exist until we act. If you thought about stealing something from your employer, the act itself is what makes the theft an actual, instead of a potential, reality. Likewise, evil becomes real *only* as a result of someone's choice and action.

One person making a mistake with this freedom can negatively affect the lives of others. Some people choose to abuse other people, to become tyrants, wage war, or commit genocide. The 9/11 catastrophe exemplifies the potentially destructive power that accompanies freewill choice. God did not cause this nor did he prevent it. The perpetrators misused their gift of choice and hurt thousands of other people.

Why would God allow such devastation and suffering to happen? Why would He not intervene? The answer is basic. Freewill choice has very few limitations. We can't use it to countermand the laws of nature; for example, we cannot just choose to time travel or shed forty pounds in a day. But we do have a tremendous range in which we can exercise this power. We have the freedom to make mistakes, to make horrible decisions. Rescinding or overruling this power, even for atrocious choices, would eliminate it from being a true freedom.

God and Nature

I came to believe that God created nature but nature is not God. Nature is the mechanical, material part of God's creation.

Earthquakes, floods, hurricanes, and many other events are just a part of the natural forces of our planet, some occurring because it's still settling from its original positions. God doesn't pick where disasters hit. With billions of people covering the planet, it is inevitable that these gigantic and awesome forces will come into conflict with humanity. People build their houses where floods, hurricanes, or earthquakes have historically struck. Others live in areas where disaster unexpectedly strikes, or they do not have the scientific knowledge to anticipate such occurrences. Then many blame God for the consequences when the outworking of natural forces causes a tragedy. This resembles having your car stall on the railroad tracks, be destroyed by an oncoming train and then blaming the people who manufactured the train. Nature doesn't have a heart or show any more compassion than would the locomotive coming at you on the railroad tracks. Neither one has feelings. Neither one is out to get you, but if you get in the way, you'll get hurt—God didn't do it.

Disease fits the same pattern. The vast majority of it originates in nature and follows natural laws. Sometimes, the cause and effect are obvious. At other times, suffering strikes innocent people for no apparent reason. Barbara, my second wife, continued smoking two packs of cigarettes a day, even though she knew the risk of cancer this entailed. She developed lung cancer and then liver cancer and she died within two years of the diagnosis. She never once blamed God or asked "Why me?" because she knew she had accepted the risk with her decision and actions.

Accidents often involve the power of choice, but they sometimes reflect the random chance that's just part of a physically unsettled world. They offer another demonstration of how one person's choice can impact another person's life. Say a man chooses to drive while intoxicated and kills a young couple and their two-year-old baby. Saying that God took these people insults him and avoids placing the responsibility where it belongs. No loving parent would select one of his children as a target for suffering. God gets blamed for a lot of affliction that is caused by personal choices and random chance.

Of course, if God is all powerful, why does He not make a world without these problems? Does this struggle offer any benefits? Yes, it does. Living in a utopia may be blissfully peaceful but that would do little good for individual or group growth or self-reliance. If we did not have to face adversity or problems, what would be the value of our power of choice and our initiative? Such a lack of challenges would stifle any drive or desire for growth.

If we had no consequences for our decisions/actions, how would we ever learn the value of correct choices? Strength of character and wisdom are forged between the hammer of adversity and the anvil of experience.

God and Death

God doesn't take people, He receives them.

Nature, accidents, random chance, the consequences of other people's personal choices, and our own all contribute to inevitable death. A loving, divine parent does not choose a specific time, place, or manner for an individual to leave this world.

The parents of the young man who died in the snow found these ideas a welcome alternative to what they had heard about God. These ideas cannot eliminate the pain that comes from such a devastating loss; they are not magic, nor are they feeling-deadening drugs. Elaine and Bob used these ideas as building blocks to personalize their own concepts. They rebuilt their marriage and family on a spiritual foundation, and eventually, they helped other people find and apply these solutions. They credit their new life to the spiritual path they now try to live.

Deiphobia

Deiphobia represents the fear of what might occur if we allow God to participate in all aspects of our daily life. Misunderstanding spirituality makes this a pretty scary proposition, and that fear blocks millions from investigating a truly spirit-led life. Deiphobia takes on many forms that appear justified from the sufferer's perspective. Let's take a brief look at some of these.

1. Thinking about God will take all the fun out of life.
    Actually, life becomes much more enjoyable and exciting when it's based on a personal spirituality. It's not

at all dull or boring. A devoted parent wants His children to benefit from all fulfilling aspects of life on this planet. This includes enjoying health, work, laughter, and fulfilling relationships with family and friends. It also includes learning to use our endowed physical, mental, and spiritual resources to overcome challenges, and to enjoy fantastic sex. That's right, I mentioned sex. Spiritually motivated sex elevates that physical union to an entirely new and beautiful experience.

2. If I give up my personal self-will, what will be left of me?

Many people feel concerned that, if they let go of their personal will, they will become non-entities, like the holes in doughnuts. This does not happen. Spiritual living involves consecrating our will—not relinquishing it. Willpower can be a valuable asset because aligning it correctly produces a better life. This means aligning it with universal forces, going with the natural order instead of against it. We do not give up our will. Instead, we choose to align it with a higher purpose instead of having it motivated by self-interest. We consecrate our self-determination to follow the best plan for our lives. Using and rededicating willpower is vastly different than simply trying to live without will.

3. I can't live up to the expectations of this kind of life.

Many of our expectations are self-imposed and not dictated by God. Even if we follow a spiritual path for years, we are still spiritual babies. We will make mistakes, but that's not a big deal if we learn from them. In fact, mistakes often give birth to wisdom.

4. I have a few problems, but generally I'm all right. Why consider changing?

Good is often the enemy of *best*. Remember the Fassell analogy about the frog that will remain in gradually increasing heat until it dies? You may be settling for misery and mediocrity without being aware of how wonderful life can really be. If you worry, feel anxious, or need a pill or a drink to relax or socialize, if you watch television more than you play with your children or spend time with your spouse, you can definitely enjoy a better life.

If any of these block your acceptance of spirituality, becoming a little open-minded to this groundbreaking process can open new doors. The transformation and resulting attributes of the Phoenix People demonstrate that it really is this simple.

The Faintest Flicker

I've come to believe that each of us has an inner spirit of truth that helps us recognize the truth when we're looking for it. This is the inner part of us that resonates when we have an *aha* moment or when something we read, hear, or see strikes a responsive chord. It's like an inner tuning fork. These experiences were pretty rare when I started this journey, but they have become more frequent as I learn to provide fertile ground and opportunities for them to occur.

I was camping in a large valley on the South Buffalo Fork River in a wilderness area of Wyoming. I pitched camp in a golden aspen grove and enjoyed the fall twilight. I could see almost two miles up the valley and almost a mile downriver. Deepening clouds threatened a thunderstorm before morning. I checked the horses, read for a while by lantern light, and went to sleep. A few hours later, I awoke to an awesome light-and-sound show, rarely experienced in the lowlands. Thunder bounced off the mountains and rolled across the valley; lightning flashed brighter than any Fourth of July fireworks. I could see the horses in the bursts of light and I knew they were doing fine. After the storm passed, I went over to them, checked everything, and calmed them down.

Walking back to my tent, I switched off my light and observed the absolute blackness. Somehow civilization makes me forget the impenetrable darkness of a moonless night in the wilderness. I'm repeatedly surprised by the complete absence of light.

The valley was totally black, not even a hint of light in what had been a two-mile vista before dark. Then I remembered a phrase I had read that said, *God ever responds to the faintest flicker of faith.* Standing there completely alone, I scratched a match to flame. Seeing this little bitty flame in the vast darkness gave that saying a deeper meaning. I held in my hand the only source of light for miles. This simple statement told me that, if this flame represented a feeble attempt at faith, God would find it and respond to it. I realized that it was even better than that. If I had a barely perceptible flicker and the entire universe was in darkness, He would even find and respond to that. Wow! Pretty awesome. I stayed up for over an hour thinking about that, but I slept like a baby when I finally turned in.

Developing a Spiritual Relationship: Implementing the Solution

"Neither shall they say, Lo here or Lo there! For behold, the kingdom of God is within you."

—Luke 17:21
21ˢᵗ Century King James Translation

I was dubious when I started investigating this spiritual power. After all, it wasn't something I could see or measure with scientific instruments. Then, I realized that I readily accepted other forms of energy that I can't see. Anyone who has witnessed the devastation of a hurricane or tornado easily accepts the power of the wind. We can't see the wind, but we believe it has power because we observe its effects on other objects.

The same is true of electricity. I previously mentioned this, but additional discussion will help expand the analogy between these two powerful invisible forces. I can't actually see electricity. I see the results it produces on other objects, such as light from a lamp, heat from the stove, and the fan turning. Observing these predictable results leads me to accept electricity as a real power. Now, I can measure electrical energy with physical measurements of voltage or current, but I can't do that with spiritual energy because it's not a physical force. So I have to evaluate this power solely by the results it produces. If studied properly, these results are verifiable, measurable, and reproducible. For someone like me who resists accepting things I can't see, comparing spiritual power to electricity can bring an understanding of this invisible force.

If I have a lamp that I want to light a room with, I have to do a couple of things to make it work. I must plug it into the electrical outlet and turn on the switch. I can want to see the light with all my will and determination; I can sit and watch the lamp, wishing and praying with devout zeal for the light to appear. But I will get zero results if I don't connect the lamp to the power source and turn on the switch.

I'm glad I don't have to understand the theories of electricity, how electrical power is generated, or how it flows down the transmission lines and gets into that little outlet in the wall. I may be the quintessential skeptic and not believe in the power of electricity; however, if I take the right action, the light from the lamp will still illuminate the darkness. *The results depend on my decisions and actions rather than on my belief or understanding.*

Spirituality works in much the same way. The required action is similar to getting the lamp to work. All we have to do is plug in, turn it on, and enjoy the results. This means we have to access the spiritual energy that resides inside every one of us. This reservoir of power sits there waiting to do its work, to help us, just like the electricity that flows behind the walls of our home. However, each of us has to make the connection and then keep the circuit open to let this energy flow. Whether it's electricity or spiritual power, the life-changing energy cannot yield benefits without the connection between the need and the power source. While we utilize electricity with a physical connection, our spiritual relationship becomes the conduit by which we tap into our inherent spiritual energy.

This association forms and grows like any other. It is an individual experience that can be different for each of us, but it moves through specific stages, like any personal relationship. They start with an introductory stage where we first meet the other participant. At this time, we don't have a lot of trust or expectations. We're not committed and we have a minimal emotional investment. From there, if we choose, we may move into the friendly stage. We spend a little more time together and communicate more. We share history, values, outlooks, and ideas. The friendship deepens. Trust, commitment, and support increase. We are there when our friend needs help and we expect a similar response from them. We feel that the other person won't judge or reject us, that we have the freedom and safety to share just about anything with them.

The spiritual relationship works the same way. It takes energy, time, and commitment for it to move into deeper levels. If we want to go deeper, we may need to develop an understanding of what is God's part and what is our part in this friendship and cultivate new communication skills.

God's Job

In the previous chapter, we looked briefly at some of the misconceptions about God. Now, let's clarify God's role in this relationship. This is not an attempt to define God or everything he will do; however, we have to have a starting point. We need a basic understanding of God's role because if we expect God to do something that he's not about to do, we set ourselves up for disappointment. Then we may reject the total concept of spirituality because we expected the wrong things. Likewise, we should understand our responsibility so we don't expect God to fulfill our obligations.

Whether we're thinking about spiritual power or the most efficient way to do any job, most of us are interested in action and consequences—what produces results. What specific results can we anticipate in this spiritual area? Objectively answering this requires that we fall back on the scientific tools of observation, experiments, and verifiable results. The observed results also have to be *repeatable and consistent* to enhance confidence in the association between action and outcome.

In my adventure of using these evaluation methods, talking with thousands of people walking this path, and personally experiencing the effects of this power, I've reached a few conclusions. These are not concrete, and they will likely expand as I understand more, but they do represent basic concepts that yield reproducible and dependable results. Each of us should observe and verify our own conclusions as we see results from this developing relationship.

I've seen no consistent evidence that God will help us hit the lottery, get rich or famous, or do a number of other things that some people believe. However, I have observed definite results from this spiritual relationship. When we begin this journey with sincerity, God delivers some amazing gifts:

- He gives us access to a pre-existing, in-dwelling power, a very real form of energy that opens a new dimension to life.
  - o This added depth produces a higher quality of living. It generates life experiences that are unfathomable and unattainable without this energy.

- o This energy produces self-actualization and spiritual transformations.
- o This is the power that breaks addictions, removes old patterns, and casts aside all shackles of the past and fear of the future.

- He supplies us with guidance.
  - o Our developing inner compass guides us toward better decisions, which improve our life. This direction sometimes comes not as a thought, but as a hint, a feeling, a slight inner tug that one path is the better choice.
  - o Our values, principles, and goals shift to a higher plane.
  - o An exo-centered life replaces an ego-centered life.

These two major gifts combine to yield highly desirable benefits.

- We enjoy a sublime peace which surpasses all human understanding.
- A sense of security and well-being pervades our entire existence. We understand that no matter what happens on the outside, no matter how badly the exterior shakes and crumbles, we are protected and loved and will eventually rise above all concerns.
- We are invigorated with an ability to face and conquer the vicissitudes of life, overcome the daily challenges of living, and transcend the inevitable disappointments and pain. And we do all this with equanimity, peace, and love.
- We intuitively feel a connectedness with others. An absolute certainty of our place in humanity replaces our feelings of isolation and loneliness.
- An altruistic desire to help and serve others infuses us. We want to share this awesome life with anyone who wants to experience it. We respond compassionately to the needs of others.

God does what we cannot do, but He will not do what we are able to do.

Our Job

Okay, we've looked at what we can realistically expect God to do in our life. Now, let's look at the other end of this partnership. God is pretty good at doing his job, but he is not going to do ours. If I lie on the couch and pray but refuse to work, I will be disappointed if I expect him to deliver food to my door as the result of my prayer.

Developing a spiritual relationship is simple. We don't have to believe in or understand anything to start—we only need to be open-minded enough to try. We make the decision and take the action, work the described process. Then, we experience the results. We recognize and acknowledge the changes in our lives and use these verified results to build and enhance our own ideas and conclusions.

After our initial decision, the first action is learning to communicate. This takes a slightly different form in the spiritual relationship. We're communicating with a silent partner, someone who rarely speaks audibly. We start this by mentally talking to our inner guide. This isn't a long-distance effort; our prayer doesn't have to carry into the galaxies but just to the spiritual presence that resides within each one of us.

Children offer some great lessons about prayer. My neighbor Mike had been teaching his fourteen-year-old son to drive a car on backcountry roads. One day, Mike and I were drinking coffee when his son came in. Mike Jr. asked if he could drive his friends to town. Of course, his father told him no, that he had to wait until he had a driver's license and insurance. The boy got angry and petulant, saying that he knew how to drive and he should be allowed to go. He sincerely thought his request was reasonable, but as his parent, Mike had to say no.

My immature prayers have, at times, resembled this type of request. I used to give God a "wish list" or tell Him what *should* happen. I used a lot of *foxhole prayers*, promising "If you get me out of this one, I'll never do it again." I was asking God to prevent the consequences of my actions and give me what I wanted. Essentially, I tried to get him to align his will with *mine*. I wondered why my prayers went unanswered. Or if I got the results I prayed for, by some random occurrence, I went to one of two extremes. I either assumed it was luck and had no connection to God, or I made a link and let it reinforce my ineffective pattern of prayer. I used a few chance results to justify my erroneous ideas about how God responded to prayer.

A little more maturity helped me understand that, often, certain laws and natural forces control the answers to prayer. God will not cancel these forces just because I want something or have done something stupid. If I decide to jump from the top of a ten-story building and commit suicide, God will not stop me. If I jump and then change my mind at the eighth floor, prayer will not alter the consequences. I can pray with all my heart, but I will still splatter on the sidewalk. God won't suspend the law of gravity because of my poor decision.

However, if I sincerely ask for help when making my decision to jump—*before taking the action*—God will definitely respond. He'll provide an opportunity to make a wiser decision. The turmoil inside will lessen; a view will resonate within me or someone will suddenly appear to talk with me. *Something* will occur that will help me see things from a different perspective. I still have the power to choose either path, but God quietly offers me a more beneficial alternative.

That is exactly what happened to me when I almost committed suicide. In extreme anxiety, I pleaded for help but didn't believe that I would receive an answer. Yet, a thought appeared in my mind that seemed to come out of nowhere. It burned itself into my consciousness and gave me a chance to change my course of action. Since then, I've talked with hundreds of people who've had similar experiences.

An abrupt total loss of my eyesight provided another opportunity to test these theories on prayer. In 1994, rare bacteria invaded and destroyed both of my corneas, leaving me completely blind. Fear of indescribable magnitude controlled my mind and my soul. I was blind! No specialist could predict whether or not I would regain my sight. For the first two days, I desperately begged God to heal me. Thoughts of, "How can I work and support my family if I am blind?" and "How can I enjoy anything about life without seeing?" dominated my mind. Then I remembered the principles I had learned about effective prayer. I sincerely and unreservedly asked God to help me accept everything *just as it was at that moment*, to help me understand that I could be a useful person even if I was blind and to help be receptive to divine direction in this situation. My vision did not miraculously return, but within hours, I felt a profound and sublime peace that dissolved the stark terror in my mind. It was an indescribable experience to know that I might never see again and not feel worried or afraid, to feel calm serenity at my deepest level of being.

Over the next four months, I maintained the same prayer and stayed entirely free of fear. My eyes healed. During my last exam, my doctor admitted that he had doubted I would ever regain enough sight to be able to work or drive again. He said that his treatment had stopped the bacteria but medical science could not regenerate my corneas. He concluded that, somehow, my attitude had greatly contributed to the healing and that he was amazed how I went through such an ordeal with no anxiety.

In retrospect, I saw that when I gave God my fear-driven instructions of how he should heal me physically, I got nothing. I had reverted to my old method of trying to get him to align his will with mine. When I offered a more spiritually mature petition, I received definite and almost immediate answers.

That is an example of the *Spiritual Engineering* approach to spiritual petitions. This approach focuses on three practical applications of prayer: 1) what to ask for in order to have a high probability of getting results, 2) what results to expect, and 3) the process to follow.

Prayer is not a technique that can be used to escape from conflict, but rather, it's a stimulus to growth in the very midst of conflict. If we have severe economic problems, for example, prayer will not help us hit the jackpot at the casino, but it can bring peace of mind and help us focus our mental abilities. This allows us to find the best solutions for our own problems.

If we are heartbroken from a relationship, prayer will not force the other person to respond to our wishes, but it can change us so that we become a better partner and form relationships based on love rather than on need. If we suffer from an illness or a handicap, prayer may not miraculously heal our bodies, but it will bring the serenity that drives out fear. This peace, in turn, gives our wonderful body the best chance to heal itself.

God is not Santa Claus, nor is prayer a Christmas list. Effective prayer requires some groundwork:

1. We have to courageously face the inevitable challenges of life. Prayer cannot be used as an escape mechanism.
2. We need to exhaust our human capacity to solve the problem—to be industrious and use all the resources at our disposal
3. We must recognize that we cannot solve the problem relying on our physical, mental, and self-willed resources. We accept that we need additional help.
4. We must progress to that place of spiritual maturity wherein we align our self-will to the transforming embrace of spiritual growth. We ask for direction instead of giving direction.

With these guiding principles as the foundation of our prayer, the results will correlate directly to the spiritual maturity and wisdom of our petition.

What to Pray For

As our divine parent, God is primarily interested in our spiritual well-being. If he answers any prayers, we should expect direct answers in this area. Of course, a spiritual answer significantly influences all areas of our lives.

I have learned to pray for values, not things, and for growth, not gratification. Asking God to solve our difficulties dishonors our own gifts of thought, free will, and our ability to work and realize the results of our efforts; however, we can always ask him for wisdom and strength to guide and sustain us as we courageously deal with the problems at hand. Mature prayer is fair-minded—it never seeks a selfish advantage over our fellowman. Our spiritual bond will grow and mature as we modify our communication. Listed below are seven ideas that we might consider.

- Request knowledge of God's will (or universal principles) and how to understand and apply these in our specific situation.
- Ask for direction for our minds. Begin by acknowledging that most of our problems and solutions lie in our own minds. Then we concede that we cannot enjoy life when self-driven will dominates our mental outlook. Thus we seek help in directing our thinking. We might ask that:
  o love replace our selfishness;
  o thoughts of helping others grow while self-centeredness fades;
  o faith melt our fears;
  o understanding displace our anger;
  o spiritual growth replace our guilt;
  o humility shrinks our ego;
  o gratitude diminishes our anxiety and self-pity; and
  o our actions become more divinely motivated.
- Appeal for willingness to persevere in this spiritual journey. If we have difficulty in any aspect of spiritual growth, we can pray for the willingness to be willing.
- Pray that we might have increasing receptivity to our inner spiritual leadings; that we learn to discern the difference between divine will and self-will.
- Request spiritual progress for our loved ones, for humanity, and for ourselves.
- Seek guidance in solving specific problems. We can lay out our needs before our guide and ask to be given the wisdom, strength, and guidance to acquire the best resolution.
- Ask for help in overcoming character traits that impede our spiritual growth or negative feelings that detract from happiness.

Results of Prayer

Prayer is not meant to change the divine's attitude toward us but rather to change our attitude toward the divine and other people. We, not God, are the ones who need to release the shackles that hold us in bondage. We are the ones who need to develop our understanding, ennoble our purpose, elevate our intellect, and consecrate our will. Prayer opens the human end of the divine–human communication channel and then expands this conduit. This allows us to receive the wonderful gifts of spirit that are always waiting to be distributed but can only flow in direct proportion to our capacity to receive. A twelve-inch-diameter water main can stream more water than a half-inch garden hose; a larger spiritual pipeline lets the blessings flow more easily and abundantly.

Prayer lets us receive more and become increasingly aware of its results in our daily life. Sometimes these results are more subtle than obvious. They often appear as:

1. A change in attitude or perception

    If someone irritates us, prayer may not move that person out of our life, but it can change our outlook toward him or her. We may read or hear something that enhances our understanding of that person's motives, or we might find our self becoming more tolerant.

2. An insight

    Mental and emotional calmness often precipitate a sudden understanding of a principle or concept that makes our life more meaningful or worthwhile. This can move us to a higher level of comprehension that, in turn, rearranges many ideas and reactions in our life.

3. Opportunities for growth

    Often, instead of granting us specifically what we asked for, prayer gives us a chance to achieve it. The spiritual domain provides the opportunity to learn—plus the strength to accomplish the objective and the inner reassurance that we can do it. For example, asking for patience may not make us a shining example of patience overnight, but it may provide multiple chances to practice this attribute. Persistent prayer also provides the power to overcome material, mental, and emotional obstacles that may block our path of spiritual growth.

4. Guidance

When facing a decision, we may experience an intuitive feeling that one direction is better than the alternative; we may see an underlying motive that helps us honestly evaluate our options and discern a better way.

5. A progressive mental maturity that yields a number of benefits:

   ○ *Peace of mind, the feeling that all is well.* We discover the ability to match calamity with calmness and feel the certainty that everything will work out.

   ○ *Enhanced mental clarity.* We become able to see answers that previously eluded us or develop skills to eliminate the mental clutter that obscures solutions. Our mind becomes more focused and our mental efficiency greatly increases. We experience fewer problems and find easier resolution to challenges and conflict.

   ○ *Increased awareness that certain habits create misery in our lives.* This may lead to a commitment to replace them with higher levels of behavior.

   ○ *A new consciousness of being able to choose an alternative way of acting or reacting.* We may realize that we don't have to allow other people to dictate our feelings, that we now have a choice and the tools to implement our decisions.

   ○ *An increasing ability to view uncooperative and abrasive people as teachers*, to see that each of them provides an opportunity for growth. We might also see that this world contains a large supply of such teachers, of people who might irritate, offend, or initiate feelings of misery in us. When we start this path of growth and maturity, it seems as if these people may be the tools by which we learn a needed lesson or may provide chances to practice specific skills. It is obviously easier to learn our lesson or develop our skill from the first such teachers we meet rather than being stubborn and repeating the need for the same lesson over and over.

The Process to Initiate and Nurture the Spiritual Relationship

Our attitudes and patterns of a lifetime do not always change overnight. A consciousness of our indwelling spirit and inner energy may happen suddenly or develop slowly. Either way, it is certain to emerge if we follow the process.

What would you do if someone offered you a hundred dollars every day if you spent twenty minutes reading a certain book? Would you do it? How many days would you skip reading? Instead of money, using this approach to a spiritual relationship offers a way of living that can transform your entire life. It can help alleviate the symptoms of misery and provide a method for having fulfilling relationships —great payoffs for a small investment.

We begin to recognize that the minutes and hours we have each day are a precious resource. Once we spend a segment of time, it is gone. The things for which we trade our time affect our quality of life. If we spend too much time making money, we may sacrifice relationships; if we spend time worrying, we squander the moment we are in right now.

Starting or enhancing our new life often means that we replace some old habits with new ones to produce different results. The process is relatively simple; it makes no difference what you believe about spirituality or whether you think it will work or not. There are no shortcuts but consistent and persistent repetition always produces results.

Spiritual Engineering Practice Session

Daily meditation books can be very helpful. If you don't have them, go to a bookstore and find some that appeal to you. Each morning, read the thought for that day, reflect on it, and see how it applies to your life. Then, close your eyes, relax, and establish that communication channel with your inner partner. Try closing your eyes for a few moments, taking a deep breath, holding it for ten seconds, and then exhaling *very slowly*. Exhale gently saying the words "Peace, harmony, relax, relax." Extend these words and the exhalation as long as comfortably possible. Feel the tension and misery leaving your body with each breath. With each molecule of air that's released, your heartbeat slows down and your muscles relax. Repeat these three or four times until you feel peaceful. Then, quietly connect with your indwelling spiritual power.

Start by acknowledging gratitude for some of the good things in life. We can always find something to be grateful for if we try. Then, mentally talk to that inner presence. Be honest. Lay out your needs and desires before this friend. Ask that your mind and motives be spiritually directed. When finished, spend a few moments in silence. You'll start seeing amazing results as this new attitude is carried into your everyday life.

Starting Your Day Exercise

- Read your daily meditation.
- Take three relaxation breaths.
- Close your eyes.
  - Give thanks for your awareness of your inner power.
  - Ask that your mind be spiritually directed—that healthy love replaces selfish and self-centered motives.

- Ask for guidance for any decisions made this day and strength to fulfill that guidance.
    - Include your personal request.
  - Spend a few moments in quiet receptivity.

If you feel upset or anxious during the day, pause and re-establish this connection with your inner power. This requires only a few minutes; do this as soon as you become aware of the problem. A campfire is much easier to extinguish than a blazing forest fire; upset emotions are easier to alleviate when they're small. Close your eyes for a moment, take three relaxation breaths, and mentally do the following exercise.

During the Day Exercise

- Tell your inner friend and guide that you need help.
- Acknowledge that you have tried but cannot get your thinking back on a healthy track.
- Ask your inner power to:
  - help you understand why you're reacting this way;
  - give you guidance for any decision you face;
  - direct your thinking into beneficial channels;
  - show you what loving action you must take to feel better;
  - relieve these feelings so that you may be of service to others.
- Declare that:
  - It is my will that your will be done;
  - I know that You will help me;
  - Thank you.

Stay a moment in quiet receptivity to give yourself the gift of silence and allow your inner power to work inside of you.

Many of us face hectic, fast-paced days. How do we discipline ourselves to slow down for a few minutes? I've learned to use anything that can increase my awareness of my spiritual life or get my mind thinking along more peaceful channels.

For example, a simple wristwatch has helped me find that elusive peace of mind during some chaotic days. It has an alarm that I've set to go off five times throughout the day. When the alarm rings, I close my eyes and take three deep relaxation breaths. I sit in appreciation of the inner quiet for some seconds. Then, I ask that I be aware of the divine spark within me for the next few hours; I acknowledge gratitude for the day, even though it may be hectic and pressure-filled. In my case, I can see and breathe, so it could be worse. I ask for guidance and strength to speak, think, and act lovingly. The full process takes less than two minutes. Experience has proven that these minutes change my whole day. This exercise represents a proactive measure and often prevents the symptoms of misery from arising.

Then, as I go to bed, I've found it helps if I spend a few minutes reviewing my day. I try to do this as soon as I lie down. This not only helps me spot areas where I didn't do as well as I might have, but it also helps me fall asleep more easily. It focuses my mind on growth instead of the fruitless rehashing of a day's events, unrealistic fantasies, or worry about the days to come.

Nightly Review Exercise

Close your eyes and relax. Take three relaxation breaths.

- Conduct your review:
  - Were you loving?
  - What symptoms of misery upset your day?
  - Were your decisions selfish, self-righteous, or self-centered?
  - Did your thoughts, feelings, words, or actions compromise your integrity?
  - If something upset you, did you have a bad five minutes or a bad day?

- o Did you pause and pray?
- o Were your fantasy thoughts—those daydream diversions—loving, altruistic, and tolerant, or did they reflect self-driven will?
- o What could you have done better?
- Review and acknowledge your improvement. Were there times when you had an opportunity to fall prey to misery but didn't? Did you do something good, kind, and loving? Did you avoid or indulge less in an old pattern of behavior?
- Give thanks for the help received that day. Acknowledge your shortfalls and make a commitment to try to do better tomorrow.

It may take time to completely break some of our negative patterns, but don't become discouraged. Remember that action, not belief or knowledge, drives and maintains the change. Knowing what we should do yields zero results unless we act.

God and Lady

I began my search for practical spirituality as a skeptic. Diligently looking for what worked and what didn't, I sometimes had insights as I spent time in nature. One time after riding Lady, my mare, out of the backcountry, I realized that I trusted my horse more than I trusted God. I hate to admit this and it sounds almost sacrilegious when writing it, but it's true. Lady was an experienced mountain horse that was thoroughly dependable. As we spent time together traveling isolated mountain country, I learned to rely on her experience and abilities. I began to take this trust in her for granted, and sometimes that put us in precarious situations because I knew I could depend on her to help me get out of them.

One day in late October we were riding back to the trailhead and I realized I had stayed too late in the backcountry. We were miles from roads, phones, or any kind of civilization. It was snowing a little and the heavy cloud cover and tall pines around us made it so dark that I had to ride with a hand in front of me to prevent limbs from hitting me in the face. I could not even see Lady's head, or anything else, up, down, or sideways. Everything was black.

I knew from memory and sounds that we were approaching a place where the trail was very narrow. For a hundred yards, the trail had a steep bank on one side and a sheer drop of over two hundred feet to the river on the other side. If Lady slipped or went over the side in the darkness, I would be badly hurt or worse. I had to trust her instincts and let her take me to safety.

The sound of the river's rushing water let me know where we were on this part of the trail. I kicked my feet out of the stirrups and let Lady have control. She never slowed down or missed a step. She just followed the trail and took us safely back to the truck. I never even had a second thought or a doubt that she would do it. We had ridden that trail many times, and I simply trusted her judgment and ability. In retrospect, this trust was not something that came with the horse or developed overnight. I hadn't trusted her like this when we first went into the mountains together, but I *slowly* came to appreciate her abilities and totally rely on her instincts in precarious situations. In other words, she earned my trust through our experiences together.

I had started my spiritual journey long before I bought this mare; however, I learned to trust the horse before I learned to trust God. Lady's dependability was on a physical level, something I could see. As I trusted her to do something, I could verify the immediate cause-and-effect results. For example, when I let her pick our trail back to camp or to the trailhead, she always chose the correct way. I knew that she wasn't going to take over if I didn't let her. I held the reins and the control. She would only do what I let her do. It took me much longer to verify God's dependability in my personal life because I had trouble seeing the action–consequence link. It also took me some time to accept that I have freewill choice with God the same way I did with my mare. He doesn't take the reins away from me and he will only participate in my life as much as I let him.

It has taken me years to trust God with my life as much as I trusted that mare. Sometimes I still have a problem trusting him. I seem to set aside certain areas of my life that I don't want him in. I think these areas are for me to control and manage, and, of course, these are also the areas that cause me the most discomfort and misery. If I have any worry, stress, anxiety, anger, fear, resentment, or guilt, then I am not trusting God as much as I trusted my horse. I felt none of those feelings when she brought me down the trail that night. I simply trusted her with my health, my well-being, and, actually, my life. I trusted her to take me through some perilous territory when I could not see the path, what was around us, or even the next step ahead. This is real trust, the type I need place in God

Today, I try to check my life regularly to see in what areas I hold a pseudo trust, areas wherein I say I am trusting God to help me but then follow my own path. I ask myself if it is my job, my finances, relationships, my future, or another area that I am keeping for myself, still holding the reins to act as the guiding force? Do I say I am allowing him in but actually keep him at arm's length from this private domain? Am I keeping him just outside the door where he'll be handy if I need him? Do I tell myself that these areas of my life are personal—that I shouldn't concern him with them? Or do I feel if I let him in, I may see answers I don't like? Do I have the trust and confidence in his guidance that I had in my horse on that dark night? Will I go where this inner leading takes me even when I can't see the path ahead?

I can fool myself about these areas I keep from my spiritual guide. I have to continually appraise my relationship with my inner spiritual force and with myself. This evaluation occurs in the self-relationship, the fulcrum for all relationships, which we'll begin to explore in the next chapter.

PART THREE

The Self-Relationship:
The Supporting Structure for
All Relationships

Developing a Healthy Self-Relationship: The Problem

"Thou shall love your neighbor as yourself."

—Matthew 22:39

The heavy glass ashtray flew out of her hand directly toward his head. John ducked and stepped quickly to the right, glass shattering against the wall behind him. He watched carefully to see if Sue was going to throw something else. In his peripheral vision he saw the terror in his eight-year-old daughter's eyes. Thankfully, only a stream of profanity, meant to batter and subdue him into submission, came across the room. Sue had gotten good at that.

The chaos settled down a little by bedtime. She wouldn't speak to him, and she slept as far away as possible in their queen bed. The angry words and *should've saids* kept John awake for hours. One voice told him that if he were a real man, he would leave and start a new life; another said that he had to stay for his two children. Then the loudest voice reminded him that if he left, he'd be alone. No one would want him. After suffering years of belittling and demeaning words, he now accepted it as fact. John just wanted to feel loved and happy instead of feeling miserable or merely surviving day-to-day living.

The relationship between them had started well, but it deteriorated over the years. In the beginning, Sue made him feel needed and wanted; she appreciated his efforts to care for her. Now they argued regularly or spent evenings in silence, and she was seldom affectionate. It was a constant struggle. John frequently felt angry and rejected. He was certain that he'd feel better if Sue would just change.

Like millions of other people, John allowed another person to control his feelings. He had relinquished power over an important aspect of his life and he had no idea how to get it back. He needed answers.

Identifying the Primary Problem

An engineering approach to John's situation works a little differently than many self-help methods. It uses the same tools on this challenge as it would any engineering or scientific task. It focuses first on identifying the root problem, then on finding the best solution, and finally on building a process to implement that solution. Let's see how this works to identify John's real problem.

You might recall that the root cause analysis (RCA) separates symptoms from problems. It allows us to systematically find the initial cause that started the chain reaction, the first domino that started everything falling. If John applied this RCA to his emotional uproar, he'd discover that his anger, worry, guilt, anxiety, and low self-esteem were *symptoms* and not real problems.

This is a critical distinction. Working on a symptom seldom solves the real problem.

Using the Root Cause Analysis would help John separate the symptoms (the feelings of misery) from the problems. As he peeled these indicators away, he would discover a shocking and likely unknown problem: John did not love himself. He *needed* other people's acceptance and respect. He depended on them to make him feel worthwhile. He had developed an inner void and depended on people and things to fill this hole. When these failed to live up to his expectations, or when he feared losing them, a symptom of misery would rear its ugly head.

Taking this investigation one step further would reveal another fact: His own choices were often the root cause of these hurtful feelings. In this case, feeling lonely and incomplete, John had initially responded to Sue's attention and demonstrations of affection. She made him feel better about himself—she gave him value. He made the choice to pursue this relationship, thus making his feelings dependent on another person's actions and attitude. Such decisions based on self—what's in it for me?—almost inevitably lead to self-fulfilling misery and mediocre relationships.

A diagram of this process looks like this:

Chart 1

Root Cause Flow Diagram

Emotional Misery
Feelings of anger, guilt, anxiety, worry, remorse, fear, low self-esteem, and others are symptoms—not the problem.

 These are caused by

Lack of Healthy Self-Love

↓ Caused by

Decisions Based on Self
Selfish, self-centered, or self-righteous motives that strive to fill the void caused by unhealthy self-love

Like John, most of us cause our own misery. We tend to blame other people, but our turmoil often stems from our own decisions and actions. Of course other people's actions impact our lives. We can be hurt, abused, and almost destroyed by others. On another hand, we can be reared in a supportive and healthy environment and then develop harmful patterns on our own. Any and all of these can contribute to impaired integrity, producing a void inside of us that gives rise to all kinds of problems.

We can't do anything to change our past, nor can we control other people today. But we can do something about our self today. To achieve personal transformation, we must focus on the things we *can* influence and control. In order to do that, we can learn to take responsibility for our present—and therefore our future. Let's take a short look now at each area of this diagram to see how this information can improve our lives.

Lack of healthy self-love

Recognizing that all relationships connect to this self-relationship is nothing new. Over 2,600 years ago, Buddha said, "Consider others as yourself." Then, centuries later, Jesus told us to "Love your neighbor as yourself." Many herald this as a path to world peace—if we just loved everybody, all would be well. However, we miss the fact that these admonitions imply *two* great truths: 1) We should extend healthy love to all people, but 2) We can bestow love *only to the degree that we have a healthy self-love.* It tells us to love our neighbor *as* we love our self. This highlights one of the major problems facing humanity today: We do love each other *exactly* as we love our self. The problem is, many of us don't have a healthy self-love, and then we're surprised when our relationships don't work out as well as we want them to.

> ### Spiritual Engineering Axiom #5
>
> Love your neighbor as yourself

This dovetails with the Natural Order of Relationships. Successful relationships don't just happen; they must be *built*. We erect the foundation—the spiritual relationship; then build the walls—our self-relationship; and finally top it off with the apex of human interaction—relationships with other people. Inherent in this logical assembly, and in the millennia-old admonitions, is the fact that this self-relationship forms the scaffolding on which we assemble relationships with other people. Every association we have with another person rests on this one. A roof cannot last long on shaky walls. Likewise, we can't build solid relationships with other people until we have dignity, self-respect, and self-acceptance, which are natural attributes of healthy self-love.

P.S/2010

There is another trait that, surprisingly, acts as an indicator of healthy self-love. It's a trait we have already mentioned, but a more detailed examination of it will show that it is one the most important factors in determining our peace-of-mind, our happiness, and the quality of our relationships. That trait is integrity.

Integrity

We generally think of integrity as adhering to a set of values or principles; however, true integrity goes far beyond this basic concept. As discussed earlier, the word *integrity* comes from the root word *integer*, which is the quality or condition of being whole, undivided, unimpaired, and complete. Lacking wholeness leaves a hole. Such a void doesn't produce a consciousness of itself but results in restlessness, an inner tension, a yearning to find something to fill the void—to find completeness and to feel better.

We are either WHOLE

or we have a HOLE

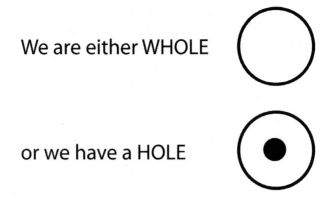

This impairment starts in our childhood. We start our life in an imperfect world with imperfect parents, family, and associates. Most of these people have their own inner void that they constantly strive to fill. They clamor and struggle, striving for more and more. This conflict negatively influences everyone they contact. When their inner conflict affects us, we respond the only way we know how: We use the same tools we see these very people using. That's all we've got, so we become like them. We damage our integrity and start creating our own inner void.

We're caught in a cycle. The hole is there. We feel the emptiness, the lacking of *something*, but we don't know what we could use to fill it and regain our natural state of unity, our feeling of wholeness. So we continue to use answers sold to us by other less-than-whole people. We load the hole with power, money, bigger toys, sex, fame, drugs, alcohol, harmful relationships, and myriad other false fillers. Each time we get our current object of gratification, the inner tension and pressure abate for a short time, but they always return because we have filled the void with the wrong things.

Okay. We have this hole inside of us that we repeatedly fill with things to try and find happiness, peace of mind, and great relationships. And it doesn't work. This is a problem. However, it's not the root problem. Even this has a cause.

The Root Cause: Choices and Patterns

The root cause is the first action that starts the avalanche, the one thing that, if we correct it, changes the sequence of events and sometimes, our entire life. In the case of our feelings and relationships, our own poor decisions emerge as the root cause of many of our problems. This may be hard to accept at first since we have spent years blaming other people or events for the way we feel. An open-minded person, willing to consider this possibility, may ask "Okay, even if true, why do we make these harmful choices? Again, this systematic problem-solving approach reveals three primary reasons.

1. We may be missing the key ingredient that lets us make wise choices for a happy, fulfilling life—a vibrant, spiritual relationship that fills our inner void with purpose, values, direction, and meaning that allows us to enjoy the best life possible, to be the best we can be.
2. We are unaware of, or ignore, the role our *motive* plays in making beneficial conscious decisions.
3. We make many *unconscious decisions* each day that dictate much of our emotional life and are never aware of making these decisions. These decisions-on-auto-pilot are extremely important to our quality of life.

A primary reason for making poor choices is that we base these choices on a foundation that guarantees misery. We accept what the world tells us is important —acquiring things, money, recognition or power any way we can. This doesn't work. Look at the results in the world, the people around you, and your own life. A house built on a foundation of sand is shaky at best and will collapse when the storms hit. We need an unyielding base if we want to build a solid structure whether that structure is a house or our entire life. Establishing an intimate connection with our personal divine spark provides a foundation that supports a life of love, happiness, peace of mind and rewarding relationships.

Now, we know that we need a foundation-for-choosing that yields the quality of life we desire. Let's look at the problems in our actual decision making process. We have two types of decision that directly affect our life: conscious and unconscious choices. First, let's examine the problem we have in making conscious choices, those decisions we actually think about and are aware of making.

We make hundreds of choices every day. Many are minor ones that just keep life flowing: "Do I pick up some fast food for dinner or fix something healthy at home? Do I shovel the driveway now or wait until the snow completely stops?" We may also face a few that we recognize as being fairly important, perhaps something on the order of "What should I tell my son or daughter about sex, or about using drugs?" Or, "Should I charge this new fishing pole even though I know our credit card bill is already too high?" Then, we have decisions that we realize may have a significant impact on our lives, and we give them a lot of thought and attention: "Do I take that new job in Dallas? What is best for my career? What is best for my spouse and children? Do I get a divorce and break up my family?"

These represent just a few examples of the conscious choices we face every day. For each one, we use the knowledge, experience, and tools we have to make the best decision we can. None of us would purposely decide to take a path that would take us into misery or keep us living a mediocre life but this is exactly what happens.

Our decision-making process often fails because we overlook an ingredient essential to making beneficial decisions: We forget to take an honest look at the reason *why* we want to do or not do something. We disregard the underlying driving force for making the choice. This effect is compounded if we do not have a spiritual foundation that acts as a guidance system for this *why* of our choices, if our motives are self-directed. Although ignored, these underlying reasons greatly contribute to the ultimate consequences that result from our decisions.

In completing this investigation, the self-driven motives—selfishness, self-centeredness, and self-righteousness—emerge as three major underlying causes of emotional turmoil. Let's examine these so we share an understanding of what they are and how much they hurt us.

Selfishness occurs when I seek something for my own advantage, pleasure, or well-being, without regard for others. It includes all thoughts, words, or actions that center on obtaining my own wants or needs, with little or no consideration of how that will affect others.

Self-centeredness represents the attitude that sweeps across all events that impinge on my life and focuses on how they impact *me*—what is their relationship to what I want, what I need, what I think should happen? All actions, all emotions, and all words are evaluated solely by their potential effect on the heart and soul of my universe–*me*.

Self-righteousness refers to overconfidence in my rightness, or being smugly moralistic and intolerant of the opinions of others. When acting self-righteously, I think I'm right and I pay little attention to other peoples' ideas or opinions. I don't need to follow directions. I believe that I either know the best answer or

I can figure it out. This attitude sheds constructive criticism and limits opportunities for growth.

These three horses plow our mental field and sow seeds of discontent and discord, guaranteeing a harvest of misery. When we act on these intentions and actually feel a twinge of guilt, our mind tells us, *Everyone does it; I'm not really hurting anyone,* or, *It's no big deal.* Actions based on these motives may produce some worldly benefit. Seen from the viewpoint of our current culture, the value of this material gain often seems to outweigh the slight negative pressure we feel inside for doing it. Then, tacit (and sometimes open) approval of others reinforces the pattern. Our little twinge of conscience becomes less and less noticeable each time we succumb to the unhealthy self-motivation.

In addition to ignoring motive, another problem keeps us chained to poor decisions and their subsequent misery. We make many decisions that have tremendous impact on our life *and are totally unaware we ever made a choice.* This is an extremely important point. Years of use and experience have moved this part of our decision-making process to the unconscious level. It has become an ingrained pattern of emotional response.

For example, someone offends us and we get deeply angry. We feel the anger and immediately react. We withdraw or lash back with words or actions. The result may seem instantaneous, but we actually go through at least three steps that lead to the feeling:

1. The event happens.
2. The event triggers an unconscious evaluation about how the event affects us.
3. We respond with a programmed physical, mental, or emotional reaction.

This unconscious decision originates from an entrenched response pattern that short-circuits our thinking process. This is the human default system that helps us make routine, repetitive decisions without wasting a lot of time or mental energy. It actually works for our advantage if it's based on a healthy pattern. However, many of us have unconscious response blueprints that we unknowingly established, that we just allowed to develop over the years. These have the power to significantly damage our lives.

When we're very young and we develop that initial hole in our gut, we fill it with something. We copy what we see our family, friends, and heroes doing. No one tells us that these initial choices begin forming patterns for our character. No one tells us because no one knows. They suffer from the same problem.

We move through life making more decisions based on selfish, self-centered, and self-righteous motives. Each one reinforces our previously entrenched patterns of mental and emotional response. The choices slowly become automatic. The mind simply does what it has done for years—it chooses the well-worn path of self-will. We're on a treadmill of misery. We don't know what causes our emotional turmoil and we can't find a way to stop it. If we do happen to recognize a potential problem, the very mind that made the initial choice rationalizes away our reaction before we get to the next level of discovery.

Thus our own decisions and actions emerge as the primary source of our misery and our problems with relationships. In addition to these basic problems, we still have one very important concept that we need to understand before we look at the solution for the self-relationship.

Free Will

On January 13, 1982, in a blinding snowstorm, Air Florida flight 90 crashed into the frozen Potomac River in Washington, D.C., killing seventy-eight people. Because of the severity of the storm, it took rescue teams nearly thirty minutes to reach the disaster. By then, only the tail of the airplane remained above water with six survivors clinging to it.

A rescue helicopter lowered a lifeline. The first man to grab the rope seemed more alert and less injured than the others. He quickly secured the line around a severely injured woman who was lifted to shore. A few minutes later, the chopper returned and again lowered the line to the waiting man. He tied it around another injured passenger and signaled the crew to lift off as the tail section slipped further into the icy water. This was repeated until only the last passenger remained. When the chopper returned for this last man, the tail section and its standing passenger had disappeared into the frozen Potomac.

The sixth passenger, Arland Williams, Jr., a bank clerk from Atlanta, Georgia, was a hero to the world. Over and over, he had made the conscious decision to save another person at imminent risk to his own life. Arland demonstrated our awesome power of freewill choice.

There are many less spectacular examples of positive use of this power of choice. Firefighters, police officers, military personnel, and others choose a life of serving others. Millions of volunteers quietly give their time and energy to help other people, to bring a spark of light into the darkness of poverty and suffering. At the other extreme are those who use this power to choose to kill, torture, maim, hurt, abuse, and manipulate other humans to fulfill their personal desires. Most people live somewhere between these extremes. They use their power of choice to lead a shell of a life, to just "get by" rather than experiencing the abundant life that lies within their grasp.

Our free will is the ultimate controlling factor on this journey to discover the root cause of our emotional and relationship problems. We simply make wrong choices for the wrong reasons and reap the consequences of these actions. Understanding the association between free will, our mind, and our indwelling spiritual guide helps us put the parts of the puzzle together to form a unified picture. We might relate it to the analogy of operating a large ocean liner. Our mind is the ship, our inner divine guide is the pilot, and our free will functions as the captain of the vessel.

Free will is our innate ability to make decisions and then initiate action based on our selections. We were given this gift so that we can build, and be responsible for, our life and our destiny. With our free will we can choose to participate in, or forsake, a spiritual life. With this power we can choose to either follow the natural way and reap the subsequent rewards, or choose self will and live a life of struggle and misery outside the universal order.

Our will operates in our mind. Decisions occur, actions initiate, and then are coordinated in our mental arena. It is ever-so-important to understand that this power of choice *also decides* whether our mind is guided by our ego (self-will) or aligned with the will of the universe (God's will). Our freedom of choice is the captain that decides whether to use the skills and knowledge of our inner pilot or ignore this guidance and risk grounding and destruction on the reefs of misery. Many times each day we face this decision point, this Y in the road. Consciously or unconsciously, we make the choice.

All of this information about lack of integrity and patterns of poor decision-making may appear disheartening, as if we have many factors preventing us from enjoying happiness, peace of mind, and great relationships. Not so. It's true that we have developed some habits that interfere with our happiness and peace, and we may not have acquired some of the skills necessary for healthy self-love, but we have made significant progress—we have identified our problem. Let's not be discouraged. Remember the powerful energy we have inside of us. That's the solution. We have all the power we need to change direction and enjoy our new life.

Developing a Healthy Self-Relationship: The Solution

"The greatest discovery of my generation is that a human being can alter his life by altering his attitudes of mind."

—William James

N ow that we know the root cause of emotional chaos and relationship problems, the solution seems straightforward. We just nurture our physical, mental, and spiritual life arenas. We develop personal integrity that allows us to love our self and other people. Life becomes incredible. It really is this simple—but it's not easy. Knowing that something is hurting us doesn't make us automatically stop the action. It takes time, effort, and commitment to following a viable process to replace old habits with new ones.

Thus far, examining our chaos in relationships and the subsequent feelings of misery, we separated the symptoms (feelings of misery) from the problem; then we identified our real problems as lack of a spiritual connection, impaired integrity and self-based decisions. Acquiring healthy self-love through personal integrity and making better choices emerge as the keys to stop volunteering for these feelings of misery. These are intertwined in actual practice and systematically solving them involves a three-part process. We learn to 1) know our self, 2) accept our self, and 3) love our self.

The First Step toward Healthy Self-Love: Know Thyself

Ancient Greeks traveled to the Delphi Oracle for prophecy and advice. The oracle—that is the actual person—changed many times over the years, but through almost two thousand years, all seekers saw the same words inscribed on the Delphi shrine: *Know Thyself.* Those two words, which epitomized all Greek wisdom and summarized Greek philosophy, never changed. *Know thyself* summarized the highest guidance of the Greek world, and it was applied whether the truth-seeker was a farmer, politician, housewife, noble, or warrior.

You might think, "Sure. I know myself. I am…I live at…and I work at…" But we can assume that the Oracle was referring to a deeper knowledge than this. Learning about our self requires that we examine *what makes our life exactly the way it is at this moment.* What thoughts, words, actions, beliefs, fears, patterns, and reactions to other people got us to this point in our life? Why do we worry? Why are we so sensitive? Why do we desperately seek other people's approval? Why do we feel like something is missing from our lives? Why do we need a chemical to relieve anxiety or to feel good? Why are our relationships mediocre?

Finding sincere and honest answers to such queries is a challenge. Nor is it always easy to know which questions to ask. This type of analysis works better if we follow a proven process. *Spiritual Engineering* tools guide us in taking a deep look at our self. We evaluate our perceptions, expectations, and motives—the how, what, and why of our existence. Or specifically, why we feel, react, and think the way we do at this point in our life.

Perceptions

Perceptions, how we view or perceive the world, contribute a great deal to our attitudes and feelings. In fact, misguided perceptions can cause us to act and react in ways that guarantee we stay in misery. Changing our perceptions can change our entire life.

As we go through a day, someone does something or an event occurs. We consciously or unconsciously evaluate the situation, form our response, and take an action. Our perception of how the event affects us—our status, our ego, our financial well-being, our security, or our love life—plays a major role in shaping this response.

If our view of what is happening is skewed—if we have a gnawing fear about the situation, if we have any bias toward the person involved, or if we are currently indulging in self-pity or any symptom of emotional misery—we may misinterpret what is happening. We see a distorted view of reality, similar to the kinds of distortions we see in the mirrors at a Fun House. Except here, we react to our erroneous perception instead of just realizing that our perception is not reality.

I once felt horribly betrayed by the other person in an intimate relationship. This untreated wound made it difficult to love and trust someone new because I did not want to suffer again. After some time, when I finally started to build another close relationship, I noticed that *perhaps* there was a situation developing in which I might again be betrayed, that I might again be deeply wounded. The more I thought about this potential hurt, the more I became convinced that I should just terminate the relationship before someone else betrayed me.

Thank God, instead of doing this, I had the sense and courage to tell the other person my concern. It was proven to me that my view of what I had seen and surmised, distorted by my fear, was completely wrong We went on to develop a long-lasting, beneficial relationship.

In addition to presenting a twisted view of reality based on our experiences, feelings, and how we got out of bed this morning, perceptions also involve a time element. Changing our timeview can often shift our understanding and response to a situation.

I used to routinely overreact to my current problems. Whatever challenge I faced at any given moment seemed extremely important—even crucial to my happiness and peace of mind. These new tools taught me to step back and see if I was making a big deal out of something that would have little long-term impact on my life. Now, I try to objectively judge if an event that is upsetting me is really as important as it seems at that moment. I ask myself, "How does this measure up to the real problems I've endured in life? Is it really a problem, or am I just following my pattern of overreacting? Will I remember it six months from now? A year from now? Or five years from now?" Experience has shown that current turmoil is often quickly forgotten. I honestly have few of what I call one-year or five-year problems—current situations that will truly have an adverse effect on my well-being a year or five years from this moment.

Look at your problems in retrospect. What specific problem was upsetting you a year ago, or even a month ago? Learning to take a long-distance view helps us see the current concern more realistically. If you're not dialing 911, it's probably not a big deal.

Asking certain questions can help us become conscious of our perceptions and develop a more accurate view of reality. When you find yourself disturbed, simply ask:

How am I *perceiving* what is happening?

- Are my preconceived ideas or opinions influencing the way I see this situation?
- Does this event truly affect important aspects of my life?
- How does it relate to my values?
- How can it hurt or help me?
- Will it have a long-term impact on my life or am I blowing it out of proportion?

Expectations

Expectations, our certitude about what will or should happen and what we believe its effects will be on our life, have a direct bearing on our feelings and our relationships. If these are not based on healthy evaluations, we set ourselves up for disappointment, frustration, or other emotional misery. Expectations are natural; they're part of being human. We can divide these anticipated outcomes into two distinct groups: healthy and unhealthy. Healthy expectations may cause pain; unhealthy ones produce feelings of misery. Remember that life gives us pain but emotional misery is optional. Avoiding unhealthy expectations significantly decreases our misery level and increases our happiness. We can learn to distinguish between these two types of expectations and develop skills that can shed the unhealthy ones.

Healthy expectations arise when we use data and experience to form an objective evaluation about the anticipated outcome. Unhealthy expectations are usually based on dreams, wishes, or projections. They may have little factual basis and only a small probability of happening.

Let's say you have done something ten times and it had the same outcome nine times. Expecting a similar outcome the next time would be a reasonable assumption and would yield a healthy expectation. Contrast this to a case in which the anticipated outcome had occurred four out of the ten times (or even worse, zero or one out of ten times), yet you still emphatically believe that it will (or should) happen the eleventh time. You believe this because you sincerely want it to happen or think that it's only fair that it happens. This is an unhealthy expectation. The data and experience do not support the conviction. Desire cannot make fantasies come true.

The word *should* often appears with expectations and that presents a separate challenge. We can have a healthy expectation that people *should* live by an implied code of conduct or by some basic moral principles, but we may want to exercise caution in this. Saying that a person *should* do any certain thing is a red-flag, warning us that we may want to examine our basis for this belief. Here are some questions that can help us in looking at our expectations.

- Do I have expectations about what the other person *should do* based on my value system? Does this person appear to share my values?
- Do I have expectations about what the other person *will do?*
- Are the outcome and its effect on me that I anticipate based on reality? Or am I looking an unlikely very worst case scenario?
- Do I have expectations about what I believe someone else will think about me?
- Are my expectations based on fear?
- Are my expectations based on facts and experience?

Let's clarify something. Prudence and foresight require making plans. Healthy expectations are not meant to stop this preparation but to guide us in basing our anticipation on facts and experience. Things go wrong—even with proper planning and healthy expectations. Random events and chance can affect our life and offset the best of plans. Proper planning just shifts the odds—the probabilities—in our favor, but it does not guarantee the outcome.

I have driven for many years without having an accident, but I still wear a seat belt every time I drive. I know that the seat belt increases my chances for survival if I have an accident. Such an unfortunate event may could result from randomity—a boulder falls of a cliff directly in front of my car. It may happen by chance—an on-coming driver drops a cup of hot coffee and swerves into my lane. Another driver or I can make a bad choice that causes an accident. Either way, my planning—wearing the seat belt—drastically improves my chances for survival.

In planning, we anticipate the *action* required. With expectations, we anticipate the *result*.

Glen, a young man attending a workshop on the self-relationship, shared his example of this:

> My wife and I had severe financial problems when a large firm offered me a temporary position for a great salary. Three months into the job, I was very busy and made a mistake that cost the company some extra money. My boss said that it was not a problem and that everyone appreciated the hard work I was doing.
>
> But a few weeks later, I noticed I hadn't been copied on some memos about some of my projects. Then the staff held a few meetings and I was not invited. Work slowed down and I became concerned that my job was in danger. I began to notice comments made by supervisors and a few permanent employees that seemed to validate this fear.
>
> I needed this job to stay financially solvent. I got so worried that I started losing sleep, and this in turn affected my work performance. Fortunately, I finally remembered the *Spiritual Engineering* tools and was able to stop allowing fear to control me.
>
> Sometime after my peace of mind returned, I received an offer for another job that presented an opportunity for me to leave. I still thought that this current position was tenuous, that I might be let go at any time, so I accepted the new job. When I informed my boss, she said that she was disappointed, that they appreciated my work, and were preparing to offer me full-time employment.
>
> My perceptions and expectations again proved to be completely wrong and diametrically opposed to the facts.

Motive

After quick examination, most of us easily accept that perceptions and expectations affect our feelings, but there is another factor that is harder to spot. This culprit hides behind a curtain of denial and justification. Motive—the reason *why* we think, talk, and act as we do—emerges as a momentous cog in our emotional machinery. In truth, our motive is often more significant than the actual deed in determining the emotional consequences and repercussions of a given act.

Let's say someone is collecting money at the office for a charity. You give twenty dollars because you believe it to be a good cause and you want to help. A week later, a similar situation arises. A colleague starts collecting money for another charity, but you don't believe that this one is as worthy as last week's cause. Then you remember that you're supposed to pick up something for dinner, but you forgot your checkbook so you're short on cash.

Giving money this time will mean that you won't be able to meet your commitment. Nevertheless, as your colleague comes around and collects the money, you go ahead and give the twenty dollars. You don't want people to think you are a tightwad, that you can't afford it, or that you don't support a good cause.

The act is identical in these two instances, but the different motives will yield different emotional repercussions. Wanting to help someone is laudable and can produce satisfaction by fulfilling an altruistic urge; giving from fear or coercion can leave us feeling that emptiness in our gut again, wondering, "Why did I do that? I should have…"

This idea of going beyond the actual deed and looking at our motive opens up new territory for many of us. We find that an act may be beneficial for one person but harmful for another; an act may induce growth one time but may retard growth another time. Here are some things to consider about motives:

1. Spiritual maturity implies that my motives progress from a self-directed basis to trying to align with greater principles—doing God's will or universal law. I can ask, "Is it loving? Does it benefit or harm others? If potential harm is possible, is it avoidable or necessary, based on my requirement that I be loving?"

2. Our motives in small, seemingly unimportant decisions start forming deeply entrenched patterns. Over time, these affect our quality of life. If we keep repeating actions based on any motive—whether this is a beneficial or harmful motive—we will establish patterns that will eventually move into our unconscious response level. Then we'll reap the consequences of these automatic motive/choice/actions.

3. Our motivation in less important decisions establishes the pattern for our response in major decisions. Thousands of small choices form patterns that determine our response in making a decision that may have a significant life impact.

4. Responding with any motive that stems from misery (fear, anger, guilt, and so on) may indicate a hidden pattern permeating many aspects of our life. Most of us will occasionally respond with harmful motives, but we need to be aware of how often these drive our choices.

Any viable solution to misery and relationship turmoil must include tools that will help us to identify these perceptions, expectations, and motives.

Accept Yourself

Self-acceptance consists of two things: 1) Accepting total responsibility for our feelings and reactions, and 2) accepting our self *exactly* as we are at this moment.

First, we must quit blaming other people for our feelings—without exception. Believing another person is responsible for the way we feel gives them tremendous power over us. It actually gives them control, as if we're a puppet on a string.

Then, we must accept what an unbiased self-appraisal (discussed in the next chapter) reveals—with no excuses or rationalizations. We must accept every good, bad, and ugly part of our self; everything that we've ever done and every dark desire that we've ever had.

Most of us don't have a problem accepting our positive qualities, although some of us may find accepting these truths a challenge. We can run into resistance against things that make us feel disappointed in our selves, or things that indicate character shortfalls. But we must acknowledge and "own" where we are at this moment. This forms our starting point for a wonderful, adventurous journey. However, we do not accept that this is where we'll stay; quite the contrary. The most troublesome aspect we discover about our self can become the area of greatest improvement.

Mike G. is an addict. His addiction jeopardized his marriage, career, and his health. After being committed to treatment centers three times, he has finally overcome his obsession for Oxycontin and other drugs. He now has eight years of continuous clean time, and he describes his experience with these different levels of acceptance:

> I fought being an addict for a long time. I had a college education and thought I was too smart to get hooked on drugs. When I tested positive for drugs at work and lost my job, I tried recovery one more time. This time I was completely beaten. I still didn't like the idea of being an addict, but I accepted that the evidence was impossible to ignore.
>
> I worked through the twelve steps and my life slowly improved. I lost that overwhelming obsession to use chemicals. I got a decent job; my wife and kids gave me another chance. After a couple of years, I could look at my addiction and be okay with it. I accepted it as a disease. I hadn't volunteered for it any more than I would for cancer.
>
> Then I realized that my life in recovery was better than my life had been before I started using. My addiction didn't bloom until after I finished college. I had a lot of *normal* time, and what I have now is much better than normal.

Then I had problems, but no answers. I still have problems, but my recovery program has given me solutions.

I would not be able to accept a spiritual answer if I had not experienced the horrible beating I got from addiction. I had too much pride and self-sufficiency. Today, I would not change being an addict, even if I could.

Once you start accepting yourself, you can start loving yourself. At first, this may appear egocentric, but it's really just the opposite. Seeing love as an active, healthy concern for your well-being helps explain the objective. There's obviously nothing wrong with having such a concern about yourself. A nourishing love of self contributes to the growth of your physical, mental, and spiritual life arenas and yields more enjoyable feelings and relationships. Learning to love yourself, to humbly and sincerely accept yourself goes hand-in-hand with developing integrity.

Learning to Love Your Self: Personality Unification, Or the Natural Order for Self

Remember, a natural order refers to the most efficient way of accomplishing a goal. The way we align with pre-existing energies and principles to reach an objective. The Natural Order of Self represents the natural order that allows us to develop integrity and healthy self-love. It outlines a method by which we can become as we were meant to be—whole, complete, and unimpaired. We start this process of personality unification by realizing two things:

- Each person functions within physical, mental, and spiritual life arenas.
- Developing into a complete, mature personality requires unification, or integration, of these arenas.

Integration of these life arenas is different than balancing them. *Balance* implies equality of these separate areas without acknowledging their different roles. *Integration* recognizes that while we must nurture all three arenas, each has a specific function in achieving wholeness. In this natural order of self, the physical life arena is *subordinate*, the mental life arena is *coordinate*, and the spiritual life arena is *directive*[1]. Our feelings act as a barometer to indicate how well we're doing with unifying our personality.

Spiritual Engineering Axiom #6

In the Natural Order of Self

1. The physical life arena is subordinate.
2. The mental life arena is coordinate.
3. The spiritual life arena is directive.

The *physical life arena* includes all physical aspects of our life. This includes our body, house, job, money, car, toys, environment, and so on. We sometimes fall into the trap of thinking that these physical elements *are* our life, that they give us value and make life worthwhile; however, these should be considered a *subordinate* value in life. Over and over, the Phoenix People demonstrate that happiness and serenity do *not* depend on achieving physical well-being or material wealth. I've met too many people like Gene, the penniless and blind ex-sharecropper I mentioned earlier, who exhibited happiness far beyond that of people possessing wealth and having far fewer physical challenges. Many of us know someone who is happy in spite of physical difficulties or limited material possessions. Contrast this with the movie star, musician, sports hero, or politician who had wealth and fame but threw it all away on drugs or other bad choices. Both extremes exemplify that physical well-being and possessions may enhance our quality of life, but they are not the primary determinant of our happiness and peace of mind.

The natural order does not denounce the material side of life. We can enjoy fantastic material gifts when we receive and use them in line with universal principles—secondary to values, motives, principles, and ideals. We don't have to be poor to be spiritual.

The *mental arena* focuses on our magnificent, magnifying, machinating, marvelous mind. Our mind stores data, receives and processes sensory input, discovers better ways to advance our interests, and evaluates alternative actions. It reflects on probable outcomes, makes decisions, and initiates action. Our mind can, and should, do all these things and more, solely on its own. These are natural functions of our ever-advancing ability to analyze, think, and plan.

However, history, and likely our personal experience, shows that left to itself, our mind can rationalize and justify many absurd or harmful actions. It can consume us with worry when we don't want to worry, lead us to regrettable decisions that it justifies at the time, or convince us that we must accept misery or a second-rate life. In extreme cases, an individual's mind can rationalize stealing, murder, rape, and genocide. This wonderful thinker of ours can take us into either emotional upheaval or an extraordinary life. Depending on the direction we allow it to take, our mind can be our best friend or our worst enemy.

Spiritual Engineering Axiom #7

Our mind can be our best friend
or our worst enemy

Again, let's look at a physical example. In this case, let's say we have a super-efficient car that gets one hundred miles for each gallon of gasoline consumed and we start a trip from New York to Denver without a map or GPS. We just start driving following a zigzag course that takes us one thousand miles more than the most direct route would take. Our mistakes in choosing a route far outweighed the advantages of our great car. We didn't effectively use our resources to accomplish our goal. Being effective implies that we achieve our objective with the least amount of time and effort.

Likewise, our mind may be very efficient, but it also needs a direction to expend its energy to effectively advance us to the highest quality life.

This is the very function of the extraordinary essence that lives within every one of us. When asked, it supplies direction, purpose, values, principles, and ideals to our mind. Then our mental life arena *coordinates* physical action with the leadings of our inner source. In such choices, our spiritual compass *guides* us to the best choice, our mind devises *how* to do it, and our body (or the entire physical arena) *implements* it. Making certain decisions without the check-and-balance of an inner authority moves us out of the natural order, and it almost inevitably produces problems and misery in relationships. When we operate that way, we are paddling upstream against the current instead of going with the flow.

The term *spiritual life arena* simply refers to where we conduct the spiritual relationship, our connection and response to our inner spirit guide, the God within. We've discussed this relationship in previous chapters, and here, we only need to note that the spiritual life arena refers to the inner realm where this activity occurs. We know that we can live an entire life ignoring or only dabbling in this concealed arena. However, this limits our potential because then we're operating in only two dimensions, like using only length and width to describe an object but ignoring its height. Recognizing and nurturing the spiritual relationship adds a third dimension to our existence—it adds depth. This also introduces a separate and specific form of energy that we can utilize to power our life drive. This additional dimension allows us to build the foundation of the Natural Order of Relationships on which integrity, peace of mind, and extraordinary human associations must rest.

Self-Will Versus Spiritual Will

When we identified the root problem in the self-relationship, we saw that our minute-by-minute choices greatly impact our feelings and attitude. Our analysis revealed that a major problem in the self-relationship is making decisions based on self-driven motives. And worse, we make many, if not most, of those choices without ever being aware that we're making decisions that impact our quality of life.

This twofold problem requires a twofold solution. First, we must move the important choices we make unconsciously to our conscious level. This affords the opportunity to make better decisions. The following chapters offer specific suggestions to accomplish this task. However, when we do this, we'll still face the second part of the problem: how to make judgments that produce happiness, peace of mind, and great relationships. This is really uncomplicated. We just develop skills to align our choices with the universal will, the flow of natural energy—to make the right choice, at the right time, and for the right reason. Every decision starts us on a course that determines our resources to solve the challenges of living.

Whether a decision occurs at the conscious or unconscious level of our mind, it falls into one of two categories: Either our self-driven will directs our actions or we try to align our desires with spiritual values and ideals. This is the fork in the road and specific resources and consequences exist along either path.

Opting for self-will moves us out of the natural order and automatically imposes limitations. Acting on selfish, self-righteous, or self-centered motives produces a specific group of thoughts, words, and actions that interfere with our desired outcomes in life.

This initial choice for self-will precludes any opportunity for personality unification because it ignores the spiritual life. Unifying the three parts of our life is impossible if we're only using two parts. Opting for self-will also automatically eliminates the possibility of accessing our inner spiritual energy. Choosing self-will severs the connection to a valuable resource that we need, the force that potentially powers our inner transformation. As previously highlighted, nothing prevents us from living our entire lives in this limited way. We just suffer for it and miss the opportunity for the best life.

On the other hand, choosing the natural order opens up an alternative course. This path yields a different outcome. It establishes contact with the spiritual life arena, which unlocks amazing opportunities for a new life. Our spiritual power can function in its natural role of inner guide. This sense of direction and purpose, along with the additional source of power, provides the opportunity to unify our personality, regain integrity, and learn the skills of loving ourselves and others. This choice adds depth, energy, and direction that are not available on the path of self-will.

1. *The Urantia Book*. Chicago: Urantia Foundation, 1955.

MAKING DECISIONS

Two options exist for any decisions that may have spiritual implications or that involve values, principles, motives, purpose, and direction in life.

DECISION

Choosing self-will	Choosing God's will (Universe principles)

• Eliminates possibility of following Natural Order
• Yields a two-dimensional life
• Accesses physical & mental resources
• Impossible to fill inner void and experience integrity
• Results:
  ○ Mediocre relationships
  ○ Feelings of misery
  ○ Recurring struggle
  ○ Limited happiness and serenity
	• Opens potential to follow Natural Order
	• Yields a three-dimensional life (adds spiritual dimension) to provide direction and values plus an additional source of power
	• Gives the opportunity to develop integrity, fill inner void, nurture self-love
	• Results:
	  ○ Extraordinary relationships
	  ○ Beneficial feelings

Developing a Healthy Self-Relationship: Details of the Solution

"We first make our habits, and then our habit make us."

—John Dryden

All I ever wanted in life was to be happy. Such a simple thing. I chased money, recognition, sex, and material possessions in my search for happiness. I acquired more than my share of all those things, but none of them yielded any long-term satisfaction. I found the quest for happiness to be a paradox. I never discovered happiness by seeking it. I finally realized that happiness is a result, a by-product, of striving to unify our personality in a manner that's consistent with the Natural Order.

We are where we are. That may sound unsophisticated but it's a basic truth. As discussed in the previous chapter, each of us must deal with our physical, mental, and emotional responses *exactly as they exist today*. Most of us carry emotional baggage from the past and we've likely built some habits that hurt us. We begin this journey of self-awareness with some challenges. It's like we're taking off on a road trip from New York to Denver with a car that has two flat tires. It will be a much easier trip if we fix the tires before we move down the highway.

We need to identify what's dragging us down. Then we can move these subtle enemies into our conscious awareness and accept them. Finally, we shed these hurtful reactions. Even with all this, we will never be completely free of these feelings. We are human. However, we can all reach a place where these emotions have much less control on our lives.

Know Thyself

Remember the admonition of the Delphi Oracle, summarizing two thousand years of Greek wisdom: Know thyself. Looking at our feelings, responses, attitudes, and motives gives us a chance to do this. These are what make us what we are at this moment in our life. We need to see the real person underneath that veneer, to see what contributes beneficially to our life and what we need to chip away.

Knowing our self means that we move from a superficial awareness of our feelings and reactions to understanding their specific causes. This key part of enhancing our life is sometimes a stumbling block. Our ego spews forth endless excuses to try to get us to avoid looking at our self. It helps to remember that *if nothing changes, nothing changes*. If we keep doing what we've been doing, we'll keep getting the same results. If we want a better life, we must take actions that will yield different outcomes. It is not preordained that we have to volunteer for misery. Life can be more than a vale of tears or a routine of just getting by. Right now, let's review the most prevalent and harmful symptoms of misery. This will help us to recognize and acknowledge the ones that apply to us as we move toward self-evaluation.

Fear

I spent a lot of time in the high, rugged wilderness areas near the southeast corner of Yellowstone National Park. On one trip, I got a late start from the trailhead and had to lead two fully packed horses the five miles to camp. Walking down the trail at midnight, I heard a cracking sound in the brush ahead. I thought it was probably a young bull moose I'd seen in that area a number of times. But shining my flashlight toward the noise revealed a large, adult grizzly bear about thirty yards away! My rifle was in its scabbard on the horse and my handgun was in my saddlebags. I stood still beside my lead mare which somehow stayed calm in the face of this deadly threat. The bear just glanced at us for a moment and then rambled into the woods. After I quit shaking, we waited for a long time before heading on to camp, where I stayed awake the rest of the night.

That is an example of a healthy fear; it reflects a *valid potential threat*. The fear passes when the danger dissipates. However, unhealthy fears can decimate our life for weeks or years at a time even though they have no valid reason to exist. Our mind produces these false threats, and it is there that they live and grow. Once started, unhealthy fear invites worry, guilt, anger, anxiety, selfishness, self-centeredness, and resentments to jump into its mental cauldron. Unhealthy fear is a master of deception and denial. It breeds and incubates on a remote possibility that something *might* happen and that it will have the worst possible outcome. Some people describe *fear* as an acronym for False Evidence Appearing Real, or Flee Everything And Run.

I was astounded when I first took an honest look at the part fear played in my life. I knew that I had some financial fears, but I discovered that this deceptive evil permeated my whole existence. Subjecting fear to the microscope of self-appraisal revealed many fears previously hidden by the veil of denial. For example:

- I feared what I thought *they* thought.

  I always said that other people's opinions could not influence me very much; however, I found that I actually lived in fear and anxiety about others' opinions, which was exactly the opposite of what I had told myself.

- I feared getting caught in my little lies.

  I had prided myself in being truthful when, in fact, I engaged in seemingly harmless and often unnecessary efforts to mislead or impress people. Then I'd have a small, gnawing fear that someone would catch me and expose my exaggeration or falseness.
- I feared repercussions for participating in gossip.

  I would say or listen to something inappropriate about someone, and then I'd worry about what might happen if it got back to that person.
- I had an underlying fear of economic insecurity.

  Even when I had sufficient money, I was still anxious about "what if?" No matter how much money or how many possessions I acquired, I still thought that more would make me feel better.
- I feared the uncertainty of the future.

  I wanted to know what was coming and I wanted to be able to control my stake in it.

Anger

Anger, whether it's suppressed or acted out, affects millions of people negatively. At one phase of my research into understanding emotions, I received anger management training and taught classes to court-appointed participants who'd been convicted of family violence. Those techniques proved useful in helping some participants control their anger. However, I discovered that this practical process offered additional advantages.

I came to see the difference between the two approaches as similar to watching a bull rider at a rodeo. These fearless riders try to stay on the back of a thousand-pound plus animal for eight seconds, knowing that if they fail, the bull will try to kill them. Their physical and psychological trainings prepare them for the adrenalin-rushing excitement that comes when they ride the bull out of the chute. That's how I think of anger management now. It's a good tool to control a destructive power that will harm us. These spiritual/scientific techniques are different in that they teach skills that simply allow us to choose not to get on the bull. We don't have to volunteer to ride something that can harm us.

Many people describe anger as a normal emotion, part of the human condition. It is obviously a commonplace feeling, but we should not be lulled into adopting the norm as desirable or inevitable. The prevalence of this hurtful sensation just reflects our lack of skills in dealing with emotions. It's more beneficial to view anger as a physical, mental, and emotional manifestation of spiritual immaturity that shackles us to a lower quality of life. This viewpoint helps us see anger as an immature and potentially harmful reaction that is unnecessary and preventable.

As I worked through this process, I discovered that I had hidden my anger for many years. Honestly answering specific questions helped me see the devastation that my anger had caused in my life. I had to recognize this hidden emotion, experience the suppressed feeling, and then slowly and progressively allow my internal spiritual power to erase and absorb most of this emotion.

I still get angry, but the depth, frequency, and consequences of the anger are much less.

Resentment

Resentment is feeling angry today for something that happened days, weeks, months, or even years ago. When we see the person or remember the event that originally triggered the antagonism, the anger comes rolling back. The more we think about it, the more upset we get. The other person may have completely forgotten about what happened and be moving merrily through life, but we're still burning over it. Whether he or she did something to purposely disturb us or it was an accident makes little difference. Every time we succumb to resentment, we invite that person to control our thoughts and feelings. We give that person power over us.

Mike tells of his resentment.

> Three years after the divorce, certain things still bothered me when I thought about them. One evening I came home feeling pretty good. My new wife was working late. I had a few hours to kick back in my recliner and read a new western. As I relaxed, a thought crossed my mind about a very hurtful incident with my ex-wife and her boyfriend.
>
> I started thinking about how deceitful and manipulative she had been, how she lied to me and used me, about how selfish and unfair the divorce settlement had been and how unfair the visitation rights were. Within five minutes, I was tightly gripping the arms of the recliner. I was feeling angry, hurt, tense, and jealous again. My breathing rate had accelerated and my heart was pounding. My stomach was in a knot, and I'm sure my adrenaline was flowing.
>
> I suddenly realized that I had sat in this chair feeling very relaxed. I was in the house alone. My ex-wife was a thousand miles away, and I hadn't talked to her. I had transformed from my comfortable, relaxed state to this rage without any external influences. My thinking about

the past had propelled me from peaceful to ballistic, in only a few minutes.

Mike attended a *Spiritual Engineering* workshop and started using the tools. He continues: "I was skeptical at first. I never had been attracted to spiritual stuff, but this approach made sense. I completed the process and it actually worked. I was able to think of what had happened, of everything my ex-wife had done, without getting upset. I finally felt free."

Worry

Worry is distinctly different from solving problems. In fact, I have a 1934 *Webster's International Unabridged Dictionary* that I sometimes use to check the archaic meanings of words. It shows that worry originally meant: "to choke or strangle, to harass by biting or tearing, to subject to nagging attention, or to afflict with mental distress." Today, most of us associate worry with a troubled state of mind, anxiety, or distress. However, neither definition suggests that worry might help us find the solution to a problem.

I used to worry a lot. I'd start thinking about something and couldn't quit, sometimes letting the anxiety overwhelm me. Later, when I was free of this torture, I saw that I had believed in a force I now call the Positive Power of Worry (PPW). I acted as if worrying produced a real energy that could travel through space and make something happen, or stop it from happening. I must have also believed that, if I worried hard enough, I could make this awesome power transcend time and control the outcome of a future event. Of course, I didn't really believe this, and a belief like that doesn't make sense, but I lived as if it did.

The tools in this book virtually erased worry from my mind. They allowed me to face total blindness without worry or fear. That is a true transformation.

The more we worry, the less we enjoy life. Worry can dominate our waking moments, prevent sleep and rest, and distract our minds until we're vulnerable to accidents or lose focus on what we're trying to do at that moment. Because of the mental clutter and anguish it brings, worry actually *prevents* finding a solution. It contributes absolutely nothing to achieving results.

Jealousy and Envy

Jealousy and envy are twin branches of the same misery tree. Jealousy relates to that which I value and wish to possess and envy refers to that which my rival has and I desire it for myself. Jealousy typically refers to the negative thoughts and feelings of insecurity, fear, and anxiety over an anticipated loss of something that I value, particularly in reference to a human connection. Envy occurs when I want to have a superior inner quality, achievement, or possession that I perceive another person has. Left unchecked, either one can control my thoughts and feelings, or cause me to make inappropriate responses that create more trouble.

Guilt

Guilt is a feeling of culpability of being responsible or blame-worthy for harm or error. Like fear, guilt can be healthy or unhealthy. We experience this feeling when we think we have failed to live up to an expectation that originated from other people, from our self, or our spiritual principles. Any of these sources can foster healthy or unhealthy expectations.

Healthy guilt stems from accepting appropriate responsibility for actual wrongdoing. All of us have made mistakes that resulted in hurting our self or someone else. We really did do something wrong. It was our responsibility and we blew it. Healthy guilt can help us examine what happened, identify changes that we need to make in our approach to such situations, implement these changes, and improve our future performance. Emotional pain based on a real wrongdoing requires different tools than guilt that comes from unhealthy sources. Right now, let's focus on the unhealthy variety. Either a real or an imagined wrongdoing can trigger unhealthy guilt.

If we truly do something wrong, our reaction can cross the line from healthy into unhealthy guilt when our anguish becomes excessive, or out of proportion, to the nature of the act. This occurs when we mentally magnify the effects of the mistake, wrongly accept responsibility for what happened, or believe our performance fell grossly short, when, in fact, it was much less serious than that. We allow our feelings of distress to far outweigh the impact of what the actual repercussions are—we can accept a ton of distress for a pound of error.

The agony caused by unhealthy guilt can be based on total falsehood. We can experience these deep, soul-disturbing feelings and have done *absolutely nothing wrong*. Perhaps someone tries to manipulate us for their own selfish reasons and we respond with integrity, or perhaps we fail to live up to the standards of our peer group, and yet we know we are doing the right thing. We can be entirely correct in each of these situations and still feel the pangs of unhealthy guilt.

Shame

Shame is a feeling of humiliation or unworthiness that arises from having done something improper, wrong, or foolish. Guilt focuses on how our actions fail to meet expectations; shame also stems from expectations, but it goes a step further and attacks our self-worth.

The inner, critical voice of shame can cause great damage to our self-esteem, telling us that whatever we do is wrong, worthless, or never good enough. It may repeatedly tell us that we are stupid, selfish, a failure, unattractive, always making mistakes or saying something dumb.

Like guilt, shame can be appropriate or inappropriate, productive or counterproductive. Society, or a particular group, can use it to move us toward doing the collective will, to get us to do what is culturally or socially acceptable. Individuals (parents, peers, and spouses, to name a few) can use it to try to align us with their values. When we feel shame, we need to take a deeper look at the belief that generates the feeling. Does it reflect a value, ideal, or concept that fits the life we want to live, or are we just accepting someone else's views? How important is it? Is it a core belief that reflects the fabric of our soul? Or am I being overly critical of myself?

Here's a personal example to clarify the difference between these gremlins of guilt and shame. As I've mentioned, I had feelings of low self-worth and insecurity much of my life. They erupted into almost unbearable burdens of guilt and shame during my active alcoholism. Day after day, I sincerely promised myself to change. Somehow I sold myself the expectation that I would be successful at this, that I would do something different today and not drink. Day after day I drank, when in my deepest heart and soul I did not want to drink. I had no visible reason for drinking. I would sneak into the garage or go outside to drink, trying to hide what I was doing, deeply ashamed that I couldn't control that desire. Although I had two college degrees and great determination in other areas of my life, I couldn't turn back from the course that was destroying me. I knew I was going against my own values. I knew I was trading pieces of myself in exchange for a brief respite from the gnawing ache inside. Every drink eroded my ever-waning dignity, self-respect, and sense of self-worth until none was left. That is shame.

When I took the drink, guilt would pile on top of shame and take me to the pit of self-judgment and recrimination. Guilt resulted from the action of drinking. I wasn't living up to my own expectations, my family's hopes and expectations, and society's expectations that an intelligent, strong-willed person should be able to control a mere liquid substance.

Disappointment

Disappointment arises when events or people fail to live up to our expectations. Again, it's important to look at the history of the expectation. Is it healthy or unhealthy? Has past performance objectively indicated that we should have expected this outcome? Did information and experience justify our expectation? Or was it based solely on what we wanted—what we wished for? Remember that even healthy expectations can yield pain, but unhealthy ones always cause misery. The feeling—the symptom— is the same in both cases, but we have significantly more control over the expectations that cause misery.

Recurring disappointment opens the door to discouragement, that feeling of, *I may as well just give up; nothing turns out right for me.* Learning to avoid unnecessary disappointment lessens the opportunity for discouragement. Identifying the unhealthy expectations associated with these feelings is the first step to minimizing their effects.

Feeling Betrayed

We feel betrayed when we think someone has broken our trust. We place confidence in people, or in an organization; they do something that leads us to believe that they violated our trust; then we feel shattered, humiliated, rejected, hurt, and insecure. Thoughts like, *Why did he or she do that?*, *Where did I go wrong?* and *This is so unfair* are common when we feel betrayed.

Anytime we feel betrayed, we need to take an honest, in-depth look at our perceptions and expectations to determine if we contributed to our own suffering. In terms of perceptions, we need to ask our self a number of questions: Are we certain that the person or organization broke our trust? Could we possibly be misinterpreting the event? Are we being overly sensitive? If others told us about the betrayal, what is their motive for telling us? Are we sure we can trust their conclusion?

In examining our expectations, we need to recognize that our own emotional immaturity often makes us vulnerable to betrayal. We may blame others when they have simply done what we should have expected them to do. Let's say Paula has previously told me something that another friend shared with her as a secret. If I share a confidence with her and, in turn, she tells someone else, should I feel betrayed, or should I realize that I allowed this to happen? If she gossips about other people, should I be surprised when she gossips about me?

Our actions often put us in a position to feel betrayed. Three primary problems contribute to these poor choices: First, we make unconscious decisions—we talk before we think. Second, we act on what we want to believe instead of basing our actions on experience and objective history. And finally, we don't have a process that will help us evaluate how much or when we should extend trust. We place our confidence in people when an unbiased evaluation would show that they are likely not trustworthy. This doesn't mean that we shouldn't trust people, but rather that we need to develop wisdom and prudence in bestowing our trust.

As our relationships progress to deeper levels, we extend trust to the degree that is appropriate *based on the evidence, not on our hopes or dreams*. We find indications of trustworthiness by observing how a person acts in relationship to us and to others. Seeing that he or she has proven untrustworthy with other people should make us more cautious about extending our trust. Yet, even following these logical precautions, there will always be some people who fail us, people who, by all objective indications, we should have been able to trust. In these situations, we try to accept the fact of the betrayal and hurt feelings, use this to increase our wisdom, and move on with our lives without anger or blame.

Is It Worth It?

Remember, many of these feelings stem from emotional misery—not emotional pain. Recognizing this can offer us a tremendous advantage. With misery, we know that the symptom, the problem, and the solution *all belong to us.* Then we have a way out, independent of other people or circumstances surrounding us.

Completing my initial self-evaluation, I made a list of my primary symptoms of misery. I still have that piece of paper. As I repeated the listing process over time, I became astounded at the insidious power of these hidden patterns. I found that *I never create new weaknesses* or borrow other people's bad habits. Almost all the symptoms of misery that bother me today are only mutations of my original list. Each new life experience simply provides an opportunity to express these in new ways.

If I get sick and go to a doctor to find out what's wrong, I can expect certain things. I'll have to give a detailed description of my symptoms, discuss my medical history and how it may affect my current problem, and perhaps undergo some testing. All of this helps the physician analyze the problem, identify the source of the ailment, and recommend the most effective treatment.

Following the same logic, we recognize that in-depth evaluation of our emotional misery, knowing and accepting the root cause of our primary symptoms, will yield the best chance of breaking these shackles.

If I try to do such an evaluation using only my mind, I tend to blame others for my feelings of misery. I don't purposely do this, but when I start thinking about what "they" have done, my mind automatically tries to stop me from examining my role in the situation.

For example, I may try to determine why I was so angry in a particular situation. I might begin by taking a few steps down the path of self-honesty and say to myself, "Perhaps I shouldn't have said what I did. Maybe I was wrong in this." Almost immediately, though, before this initial thought is even complete, my mind often gives a litany of the *yeah-buts* to deflect attention to the other person. These gremlins nip any healthy self-examination in the bud and start interjecting self-justifications, such as:

- Yeah, but he had no reason to yell at me or say the mean and nasty things he said.
- Yeah, but I was only trying to straighten things out, to get her to see the right way of doing it.
- Yeah, but he had absolutely no right to treat me that way. After all I've done and put up with, I deserve better.
- Yeah, but she knows I'm worried sick about my job and trying to take care of the family. She should understand.
- Yeah, but she knows how I react when she says those things. She purposefully tries to push my buttons.
- Yeah, but..

Once I start following the *yeah-buts*, I have little hope of finding the root cause of my misery. Realizing this made me understand that if I wanted to find what was causing my emotional chaos, I had to develop a self-appraisal where I would ask myself specific questions. Asking direct questions is the best technique for ferreting out underlying problems. Over the years, I developed questions that focus on the *Spiritual Engineering* application, questions that strip away symptoms to reveal the underlying problem. This self-evaluation is available in the workbook from our website www.spiritual-engineering.com. Whichever method you choose, please realize that this is a very important part of the overall process. Mapping out the best route for any journey requires that we know our starting point as well as our destination. The self-appraisal gives each individual the clearest picture possible of where they are at this moment on their journey, a journey that continues for a lifetime.

Developing the Self-Relationship: Results of the Process

"Action may not always bring happiness, but there is no happiness without action."

—Benjamin Disraeli

I f our lawn needs to be mowed, the grass won't get shorter through prayer, magic, or hope. We have to act. Learning skills to handle the problems of life with equanimity and peace works the same way. We have to take action. Knowing our self is a key ingredient of this. That requires going beyond the superficial, abstract idea of who we are and why we feel and act the way we do. The value of doing an appraisal is nothing new. This is a mainstay of the twelve-step principles, and variations of it exist in some therapeutic practices and religious organizations.

Now is a great time for us to look at some personal stories that illustrate how this self-evaluation fits into the overall process. Hopefully, actual results will further convince you of the effectiveness of this process, as well as the need for self-knowledge.

Spirituality and the Counselor

Robert had a master's degree in clinical psychology. His twenty-five-year career in mental health included providing substance abuse counseling, being a hostage negotiator, and heading an emergency crisis management team for a large metropolitan area. He led seminars on suicide prevention for law enforcement agencies and conducted depression awareness campaigns for industry.

Over time, Robert burned out on this emotionally draining profession and he started working in the private sector. Due to a large cutback, his employer laid him off. He began working part-time while he was actively seeking a full-time job.

On the religious side, Robert had studied to be a Catholic priest for some time. He'd investigated many of the major religions, and he served as chairman of a large interfaith council.

Three months prior to our meeting, Robert's fiancée Bonnie ended their four-year relationship. Although this came as a surprise to him, for a few weeks he thought that he had accepted it and was adjusting well. Then, a combination of the unexpected breakup and unsuitable employment took its toll. He slid into depression. He said, "I was a ship without a rudder—the very foundation of my life had been pulled out from under me. I cried uncontrollably. I couldn't stop thinking of my relationship—what I had done wrong, what I could have done differently, what she had done. When I was very near suicide, I realized I was in deep trouble."

Getting even a few hours sleep required sleeping pills plus alcohol. Robert's confidence and sense of self-worth had been shattered. Despite having spent years helping other people, Robert couldn't find answers for his own problems. As he commented, "If there was anybody who would supposedly know how not to let this happen, it was me."

Repeatedly, he tried to pull himself out of this pit of despair, but he always fell backward. He was losing hope that he would ever find his way back to any degree of happiness. All of this led him to seriously consider using his loaded twelve-gauge shotgun as a way out of his misery. Then Robert attended a session where we were discussing the practical application of spirituality. He later recounted:

> As I listened to this *Spiritual Engineering* approach, I felt a glimmer of hope. What hit me at first was that this was a results-oriented process. It combined spirituality and psychology in a very down-to-earth way that just made sense. I decided to try it. I had nothing to lose.
>
> I felt like a light bulb went off in my head when we started talking about practical prayer. I had been praying a lot since the breakup with no results. I had been asking God to help Bonnie and me get back together, to help her change her mind and want me back. Every time I'd apply for a job, I'd pray that I got that job. I got zero results in all categories. I thought God had failed me.
>
> I began to see that my pleadings were self-centered. My life was a mess and I knew that some of the problems had come out of my own decisions and actions. And here I was, the person responsible for those decisions, telling God what I needed in order to get my life straightened out. I was trying to get him to do my will instead of trying to do his.
>
> When I went home that night I prayed and told God that I gave up and I needed his help. I felt an instantaneous response deep inside me, a profound shift at the core of my being. All the weight and heaviness that had suppressed me for months just lifted. I stopped hurting at once and felt free. I knew that I had found an answer.
>
> That marked my new birthday: the day I really started living. *Spiritual Engineering* made all the pieces of the puzzle fit together like nothing ever had before. My training and counseling experience had not helped me see life this way nor had my religion. I'd studied and practiced religion, but I'd never had a deep personal relationship with God.
>
> I had some initial problems with the self-appraisal. It was like hitting a brick wall. I wanted to move forward.

I could intellectually see the value in doing this, but I couldn't get started. I read the questions five or six times but I just couldn't reply. I recognized that I had a lot of resistance in this area. After praying and reflecting, I saw that I was avoiding being honest with myself. I'd always urged other people to be honest, but I found it difficult to be honest with myself. With that in mind, I was able to start.

I spent about six hours answering the questions. This was another epiphany. Many of my problems had been with me since childhood. I desperately sought my father's approval, and it was very important that I be liked and accepted. I gave other people too much power over my feelings. My early background directly influenced my attitude toward women and relationships. I also had some unrealistic expectations and not-so-great motives that caused me trouble. I had rationalized and justified these until now. Discussing this with someone who didn't judge me helped me identify the real problems and crystallize their impact on my life. Seeing how my patterns had developed and influenced my life made me more determined to change.

I had often put other people's needs and desires ahead of mine. The Natural Order of Relationships helped me see that I placed myself behind other people because I had never truly loved myself. I had made Bonnie my God— I'd placed her above my own dignity and self-respect. I had been willing to do or say anything so we could stay together. When Bonnie asked me to leave, my world fell apart.

That relationship and its breakup did not cause all of my feelings and reactions. They were the culmination of many years of not learning how to love myself and of not having a personal relationship with God.

Robert immersed himself in this new approach to living, and he gained immediate results.

He needed a job. He continued to submit resumes and look for employment while devoting time and energy to building his spiritual and self-relationships. He searched want ads and Internet opportunities, and he went to job fairs. Nothing worked out. Then, sixteen days later, someone offered him a job.

Out of the clear blue sky, an old friend called and asked me to work with him. Overnight I went from seeking work to having someone plead with me to take a job. I gladly accepted the offer and started working at a higher salary than I had ever made in my life.

I've changed the way I see and react to life. My attitude toward work, toward the people I meet, and even toward Bonnie has slowly improved. I have tools that keep the worry at bay. I prayed, and I didn't let fear enter my mind. I didn't let people *push my buttons* as much as before. I even started praying that Bonnie would have a happy life and find the love and joy I was experiencing.

I don't need sleeping pills and alcohol to go to sleep. I'm full of energy, joy, and enthusiasm. For months, I was on a natural high like nothing I had ever experienced. I now feel confident that I have answers for all the problems of living.

I met a woman who regards personal spirituality as the cornerstone of her life. We started building our relationship on these principles. We pray and meditate together. We share common values and goals, although we differ quite a lot in how we think we should achieve those. We're in the initial phase of our relationship, but I can already see that having a spiritual foundation opens new dimensions. A combination of the way we resolve differences, our willingness to discuss anything, and our commitment to help each other stay focused on these principles has given me the kind of relationship I have never even imagined possible.

The Dreamer and Practical Solutions

When Angela encountered the *Spiritual Engineering* techniques she had been using drugs for years, principally marijuana. She used them to release her feelings and enhance what she thought of as spirituality. According to her self-description, she had a good life with everything under control and was a very spiritual person. But these practical concepts, along with her desire for fulfilling spiritual development transformed her life. She reported,

> I always felt like I didn't fit in, that I had been dropped on this planet by mistake. All my family and relatives were Catholic, and I enthusiastically practiced that religion in my early years. There was a lot of chaos in our home, and I felt isolated and alone. From the time I was nine until I was sixteen, I experienced times in church where I felt close to God, and my feeling of orphanhood would melt away. I felt like I was cared for, that I was part of something big, that I had a purpose in life. I spent a lot of my life trying to recapture that feeling.
>
> When I was sixteen, I smoked pot for the first time and the experience was incredible. It gave me that feeling of being connected, of being whole—similar to the spiritual ecstasy that I had discovered in church. From then on, I connected smoking and getting high with spirituality.
>
> Over the next thirty years, I tried different religions, self-help programs, retreats, and almost anything I thought would let me find that feeling of belonging, of being whole and worthwhile. I got a degree in psychology, went to psychoanalysis for two years, psychotherapy for three years, and joined a Gnostic movement. At times, I rediscovered that sense of wonder and awe from my youth, but it would only last a short while. Then I'd have to try something else. When all else failed, I always had my drug to support me and alter my feelings.
>
> I got high on the way to church and spiritual meetings. I participated in singing, worship, and prayer, then I got

high again on the way home. And I congratulated myself on the wonderful spiritual life I led.

I had a number of intimate relationships, got married, raised a family, and did well in my profession. On the outside, I appeared well-adjusted and functional. Inside, it was a different story. I just drifted along thinking this was all life could be. A few times I had an insight that smoking pot kept me from finding a real solution, but I couldn't see a way out. I felt doomed, believing that I would continually fail to live up to my potential. I wanted to help the world, but I couldn't even help myself. When I felt down and depressed, smoking a few joints while singing or meditating would get me back to where I wanted to be.

I didn't associate with people who might challenge my lifestyle or my beliefs. My friends did as I did—they used drugs to find spirituality, or they actually used the search for spirituality as an excuse to use drugs. We firmly believed that the drugs helped us experience the most out of life.

After I got out of that rut, I was amazed at how easily I had convinced myself that everything was all right, that I was leading a good life. The drugs, coupled with my rationalization, nearly destroyed any chance that I could ever find a way out.

If we were to change a few details in Angela's earlier life, her case would fit a number of people. Instead of drugs, they might use power, money, work, acquiring possessions, manipulating and controlling people, or other behaviors to fill that inner void. They can't see how their decisions shackle their lives to misery and mediocrity. They're in the middle of a manure pile and oblivious to the odor. Or if they catch a whiff of the rotten smell, they accept it as the scent of life.

Angela continues:

> When I heard a presentation on *Spiritual Engineering*, I knew that this was what I had been searching for. Something

resonated inside of me. This combined a practical spiritual approach to life with science and psychology in such a common-sense manner that I knew it just had to work. It was so simple that I wondered how I'd missed seeing these answers before. I grasped it like a lifeline.

It became quickly apparent that I had to stop smoking pot if I sincerely wanted to try this way of life. I couldn't depend on a chemical to change my feelings—I had to depend on God. He or she was everything or nothing, had real power or none at all, would truly help me or had absolutely no place in my life. This process removed all middle ground, and it gave me specific directions on how to develop a relationship with this spiritual power and get real results. This process took spirituality from some abstract part of my life and made it the center and focus of my existence. Nothing had ever made such a clear connection between spirituality, my emotions, and my decisions and actions.

When I came to the appraisal, I hesitated but I didn't avoid it. I had to quit taking shortcuts and be willing to follow directions. I found all the questions a little overwhelming. I started with just a couple of emotions that gave me the most trouble. As I wrote down the answers and made comments, something wonderful started happening. I had never been honest about many of these things. I had kept them hidden even from myself. Writing helped me recognize certain patterns that set up my emotional responses. It helped me see why I felt the way I did and what I could do about it. I saw how misled I had been. My false spirituality had prevented me from experiencing the real thing.

Seeing the real causes of my fear and low self-worth, and knowing that I could change this gave me exquisite hope and a feeling of peace. This working catharsis was like housecleaning for my mind and feelings. Then, talking this over with a friend reinforced the relief and sense of direction I gained from this process.

I've been doing these ten years now, and I wouldn't change it for the world. This is the best part of my life. I am living the life of my dreams. I feel happy and at peace most of the time, and when I do get upset, I know that I have solutions. I have never used any chemical to alter my moods even once in all these ten years. This process teaches me to avoid many of the things that cause problems, to identify the problems when they're small, and to take action before they get too strong. I share this with other people who are hurting or searching for something. I've noticed that those who do the work get the results. Those who just want it, or think about it, get very little.

The Maid and Releasing the Past

Mani, from Sri Lanka, had worked in the Sultanate of Oman for many years as a housekeeper and nanny. She was a Christian and very active in the small local Protestant church. She found these methods by accident (coincidence? synchronicity?).

I was working in Muscat, Oman. Mani often heard when new people were arriving in the large complex through her contacts in the local housekeeper/nanny staff. If the arrival was from Europe or the US, she contacted them immediately and invited them to one of the two Christian churches in the capitol.

When I arrived, she called and then stopped by my apartment to invite me to a Christian revival in nearby Dubai. Noticing materials on spirituality and grieving on my table, Mani asked a few questions. After a short discussion on spiritual ideas and practices, we talked about how to enjoy life in spite of the bad things that hit us. I shared how these tools have helped people through grief, citing some personal experiences. All of a sudden, Mani broke down in almost uncontrollable sobbing. After I helped her quiet down and regain her ability to talk, she shared a very sad part of her life.

Mani had been married in Sri Lanka and had one child, a beautiful boy, the highlight of her life. She had taken work as a maid in a foreign country so her son might have a better life. One of the happiest days of her life was when she got accepted for the maid's position. She knew if she work hard, she could provide for her son. Like so many mothers, she sacrificed herself for the good of the family.

Her husband had a drinking problem, but he kept it under control while she was home. She knew he would get drunk sometimes when she returned to work, but her family would take care of her son until he got sober again. She felt she had little choice about working if she wanted to feed her son.

Eight years previously, Mani had left Sri Lanka after a visit to return to Oman. A few weeks after she arrived in Oman, her nine-year-old son was murdered. Her husband and his friend had started drinking. Both had gotten blindingly drunk. For some reason, the friend got so angry that he stabbed the boy with a kitchen knife, killing him instantly.

For years Mani had blamed herself for her son's death. As we talked, she revealed that she believed, if she hadn't left, her son would still be alive. Of course, she was in a financial situation where she had to leave or the family might literally starve. She had carried this guilt for years, unable to face it or shed it through her religious efforts and unable to share it with friends.

After our talk, she started applying these tools to her life. Language limitations made the self-appraisal a little more difficult, but she persisted in spite of the extra effort required. When I left Oman six months later, Mani wrote a little thank you card that made all my work there worthwhile. She said that these tools and what she had learned "*changed my life and made me big happy inside.*"

Mani's words summed it up beautifully. Anyone can learn the skills to be *big happy inside*—from an ex-counselor to a housewife to a maid. *Spiritual Engineering* is a simple, universal process that produces results—*if* you do the work.

Developing the Self-Relationship: Implementing the Solution

"The gem cannot be polished without friction, nor man perfected without trials."

—Chinese Proverb

When I started this process over twenty-five years ago, I was a driven Type A personality, always stressed out, pushing and trying to get somewhere. I thought that determination, hard work, and intelligent solutions were the answers for all problems. I was an overachiever and quite successful by many standards. But I spent thousands of days with a knot in my stomach, a sense of anxiety, and tightness in my chest. At night, my mind would start reviewing the day or planning what I needed to do tomorrow. When I finally managed to fall asleep, I only got about four-hours rest before springing awake to find myself thinking about something that would start the tension all over again. I took medications for high blood pressure, anxiety, and insomnia, and then I self-medicated with alcohol.

This state of restlessness, despair, and anxiety beat me down until I was willing to spend the time and effort required to take an honest look at myself. I didn't like what I found. I allowed other people to control my feelings. I said and did things to influence what I thought *they* thought while I appeared self-confident on the outside, I often felt *less than* or like I didn't fit in. I was definitely lacking in healthy self-love. I knew I had to accept this honest evaluation, but how do you accept a shattered reality that shows you as being so much less than what you want to be?

Accept Yourself

We are seldom what we want to be or think we should be. We may be overly hard and judgmental about our self. Our weaknesses and strengths stand exposed in stark reality and we come face-to-face with our real self. At this crucial moment, it is imperative that we move forward toward gaining full self-acceptance.

First of all, we need to have a clear understanding of what we mean when we say we have to *accept* something, whether it's our self, an event, a person, or a disappointment. It helps to understand that acceptance, of any type, does not always mean agreement. If I keep running headfirst into a brick wall and it bloodies my head, I have different ways to react. First, I can deny that I'm hitting the wall or deny that it's hurting me. Either one leads to repeating the same action and suffering the same result. Or I can admit the fact that there really is a wall there and that I keep bloodying my head and hurting myself by running into it. Once I've admitted that, there are three possible levels of acceptance.

Resistive acceptance

I understand that the reality exists, and I *bear up* resignedly, although I may believe that it's wrong or unfair.

"Okay, I keep hitting a brick wall. I don't want it to be here. It has no right to be here, but it really is here. If I want to stop hurting, I'd better not run into it."

Neutral acceptance

I understand that the reality exists and *concede* that it might have a right to exist:

"Okay, I keep hitting a brick wall. I don't understand it, but it's possible that the wall might be there for a reason, to benefit someone. I'll quit running into the wall because it hurts, but I don't like the wall being there.

Total acceptance

I understand that the reality exists and I *agree* that it is proper and right that the wall exists exactly as it does.

"Okay, I keep hitting a brick wall. I had the opportunity to view what's on the other side of the wall—a pride of lions! Now I know that the wall serves a good purpose, and I would be insane to try to tear it down. I'm grateful for the wall."

Total acceptance brings serenity and happiness, but we seldom go directly from struggle and conflict to that level. No matter where we start, we should try to advance until we achieve total acceptance

Secondly, we must accept the adage, *It is what is*. Reality does not require our approval. Most of us have done the best we could with the tools we had. Few of us have had mentors who imparted healthy and effective methods of dealing with anger, guilt, or betrayal; few of us were taught how to build great relationships. None of us set out to be miserable, yet we suffer a lot of misery. We are just a part of the human family that has slid into practicing old paradigms and accepting feelings of misery as normal.

Then we must stop blaming other people for the way we feel. For one thing, no one has the power to control our feelings unless we bestow that power upon them. And secondly, blaming another person absolutely prevents finding a solution.

For example, let's say that Marie did something very wrong and Melvin got angry at her. His perception of who caused his anger greatly determines his success in transcending that feeling and moving on with life. Believing that Marie *made* him angry gives her power over his emotions because Melvin can't feel better until *she* apologizes or changes her actions. If she is the source of the problem, then logically, the solution also resides with her.

However, if Melvin realizes that he got angry because Marie made a mistake or didn't do what *he expected*, he can retain power over his feelings. The anger is the same, but the solution is dramatically different. Solving his anger problem requires that he realize two things: 1) these feelings exist inside of him—they are his feelings, and 2) he is responsible for his feelings. No one held him down and made him swallow an anger pill that produced those disturbances. His reaction caused the feeling.

When he accepts that he is responsible for those feelings, he automatically enjoys the freedom of finding a solution *no matter what Marie does*. Responsibility means that he now has the ability to respond.

Melvin's verbal and mental communication directly demonstrates where he places the responsibility for his feelings. Does he say, "Boy, do you know what she did? Do you realize how unfair she was? She really made me mad!" Or does he say, "I don't like what she did. *I* got very *angry* with her"? The first view places the problem and the solution with her; the second directs both the problem and solution to him. Becoming aware of this deceptive pattern often brings a marked improvement in our reactions to other people.

Once you have completed your own self-appraisal, you may find that you're able to look at your list and for the first time, you will see the full cost of your decisions and your actions. At the moment when these cause-and-effect associations are still fresh in your mind, it's helpful to take a quiet moment to get in touch with your inner spiritual energy. Talk to that spiritual force deep down inside of you and ask for help. Ask to see which of your actions and attitudes might need to be changed so that you can enjoy a peaceful and happy life. This exercise often brings a watershed moment in which you truly want to release these symptoms.

Sometimes this honest examination discloses that our past mistakes caused significant harm to another person. We cannot just ignore this and blithely assume that this inner work compensates for all past transgressions. In some cases, forgiving our self for past misdeeds may involve offering restitution for harm done. The *Spiritual Engineering* process suggests that, in appropriate instances, we must be willing to face the person we have harmed and ask forgiveness; in other cases, we may have to offer material repayment. In still other instances, returning to a situation in the past may cause additional harm. Here, we commit to changing the way we treat people today and striving to avoid inflicting further damage, continuously using these tools to improve our ability to love and serve others.

We do not need to apologize for, or repair, every error we have ever committed; however, a healthy self-love demands that we cast off the major fears, guilt, resentments, and heavy baggage of our past. Remember, we would not consider starting a long road trip if our car had two flat tires. Common sense dictates that repairing the tires before we started the journey would make the trip easier and more enjoyable; however, the same common sense indicates we wouldn't run out and get a new paint job to make a few scratches look better.

We are starting a journey into a higher quality of life, and we may have to do some repair work. There is no perfect guideline on how and when to accomplish this. We evaluate each instance on its merit and consider possible repercussions to the other person and other people. We are the butterfly emerging from the cocoon, the phoenix arising out of the ashes of our previous life. We want to come through with total freedom from our past deeds, but that is not always possible.

It is essential to realize that *we must never clear our own conscience at someone else's expense.* We have no right to sacrifice our family's wellbeing to compensate for our past mistakes. Nor should we strive for martyrdom. Nevertheless, we cannot allow fear or embarrassment to keep us from taking appropriate actions. This is a delicate and sensitive balance.

We use our mind to do this self-evaluation. This is the very mind that often starts or exacerbates the negative patterns that are the focal point of this examination. For years, it has justified our actions and cited reasons why we should not apologize or make restitution.

Recognizing this self-defeating tendency leads many of us to share our responses with a trusted friend or a spiritual adviser. Such a person can help us to see and understand our perceptions, our expectations, and our motives so we can discern the best path to release the burdens we carry. A word of caution: It is essential that we choose someone who has our best interest at heart, who has our complete trust to keep our sharing confidential, and who understands our objective in this process. If no such friend is available, try a minister, a priest, or a counselor. This is an important part of the process, so wisdom and prudence should guide our efforts.

At this point, our in-depth evaluation has uncovered many things.

- We have identified our assets and liabilities
- We recognize those patterns and unconscious choices that detract from our quality of life. We recognize the power of our mind over our feelings and the fact that we sometimes cannot control or direct our thinking solely with our will power alone
- If necessary, we have started taking action to compensate for harm done to others
- We have accepted the reality of who, what, and where we are in life.

Now, we can focus on loving our self.

Love Yourself

Developing a healthy self-love requires that we allow our physical, mental, and spiritual arenas to function according to the natural order. We nurture and develop all three of our life arenas while increasingly allowing our indwelling divine essence to provide direction, values, and added power to accomplish our goals. In other words, we progressively learn and practice skills that unify our personality. The *Spiritual Engineering* method offers a detailed process of how to accomplish this. Always remember, though, reading about something, or wanting it to happen with a strong desire, accomplishes little without persistent effort—without taking action. Just like watching a football game from the stands is vastly different from being on the field and playing the game.

On a physical level, we take care of our body, our material possessions, and our environment. For example, we may need to develop healthy eating habits, get physical exercise, or consult a health-care provider when necessary, and follow through with their recommendations. If we have a habit that potentially harms our health, we commit to taking definite steps to overcome it, and then follow through. We insure that we get adequate rest, sleep, and relaxation. We look for activities that appeal to us and cultivate those interests. Do we enjoy nature? How about camping, water sports, walking, hiking, jogging, photography, or bird watching? Do we like to dance? The point is that we become aware of all physical things and nurture the areas that are important to us.

Mentally, we follow a similar path. How do we currently take care of our mental power? Do we escape through spending hours watching thought-deadening television programs? Do we relish thoughts of anger, resentment, or getting even? Do we waste mental energy in gossip, worry, or anxiety over things we cannot control? If we do, we can start to stimulate our minds with different television programs, those that cause us to actually *think* about something important, challenging, or creative. We move toward healthy, thought-provoking discussions. We may even stretch to read books by authors with whom we agree or strongly disagree. Our wonderful mind—the same type of mind that launches rockets into space or uncovers life-saving medical discoveries—responds to training and exercise, to overcoming challenges. We progressively replace mental garbage with nourishment. We strive for open-mindedness, checking facts, and looking for evidence when forming opinions and making decisions. We begin to base our mental balance sheet of other people and our self on actions instead of words, promises, or hopeful fantasies. And we recognize that our mind, like our physical body, requires diversion, relaxation, and rest.

Spiritually, we establish and broaden the relationship with our indwelling divine power. We have already reviewed some of the steps to accomplish this. Again, action is the key. Explore alternative approaches that appear attractive. Look for those that enrich and enlighten your core beliefs. Sincerely seek to understand other people's beliefs and concepts, observe the practical results they get from their practices, and consider what you want to incorporate into your own practice to enhance your own spiritual development.

Pay Attention to the Signals

As we move into this healthy self-love, we start to understand the messages given to us by our feelings, our internal barometer that indicates our progress. Performing the daily exercises and accepting responsibility for our feelings moves us to peace of mind and a sense of wellbeing. As we learn to live in the moment and shed the misery associated with past and future, we begin to experience true happiness. Life looks and feels better when we have genuine self-respect and self-love.

Unfortunately, at first we may only visit this level briefly before falling back into our familiar state of misery. Our old patterns are deeply ingrained and will repeatedly try to regain control. This doesn't indicate failure; rather, it demonstrates our evolution into a new way of life. Continuing to work through the process is key during this period. This effort helps us spend less and less time detouring into negative emotions. We are developing skills that allow us to choose whether we'll have a bad week, a bad day, or only a bad five minutes. Remember that our feelings are never about what another person is doing, or about what is happening around us. Instead, our inner alignment with the natural order, our own integrity and self-love, control these emotions. All feelings of misery are self-inflicted.

> **Spiritual Engineering Axiom #8**
>
> Misery is self-inflicted

It will take time to break some of our negative patterns completely, but don't get discouraged. Remember that *action, not belief or knowledge,* drives and maintains the change. Knowing what we should do yields zero results unless we act. We always face the inexorable effects of entropy which constantly strives to erode any unity (integrity) we achieve. Entropy will continually try to move us from healthy self-love to egoism, from following the natural order to increasing our use of misdirected self-will.

As we initiate and build our foundation and supporting structure—our spiritual relationship and our self-relationship—the door to having healthy relationships with other people begins to open. Now, we are ready to construct this apex of human associations according to a new model. This will let us enjoy those extraordinary relationships we crave.

In the next section, we'll look at the interactions with others that most of us think of when we hear the word *relationship*. As we have done with the spiritual and self-relationships, we will identify the basic problem that many of us experience in our relationships with others. Then we will consider the most effective solution, and, finally, we will outline a process to implement that solution in our daily living practices.

PART FOUR

Relationships with Other People: The Pinnacle of Human Associations

Developing Relationships with Others: The Problem

"Life is relationships; the rest is just details."

—Gary Smalley

Relationships dominate our lives. We participate in, think about, and respond to relationships almost every waking moment. They are potentially the crowning achievement of our existence. Relationships with people provide opportunities to bestow and receive healthy love, to practice tolerance, forgiveness, compassion, and mercy. Unfortunately, they can also become a breeding ground for contention and conflict, or they can simply deteriorate into complacency and mediocrity.

As we discussed earlier, it may seem that the success or failure of our relationships is based on little more than chance. Even marriage, which is often considered our most important relationship, stands in sad shape. Almost half of first-time marriages end in divorce, and this statistic gets worse each time we try it again. This occurs in spite of the fact that we may be applying the best advice available and making sincere efforts to help our marriages succeed. I'm sure that very few, if any, couples get married with the idea that they will have a family, participate in chaos that wreaks havoc on everyone involved, and then divorce a few years down the road. We enter into that union hoping that it will be a long, happy, fulfilling partnership.

So what happens? Why do so many marriages fail? Why do so many people settle for less than their dreams? And why do so many of our other relationships, such as those with friends and work associates, produce anxiety, tension, conflict, and discontent? What is the root problem here? As we did in considering our spiritual and self-relationships, we need to start with the basics.

What Is a Relationship?

I spent many years taking relationships for granted, not realizing their pervasive influence on all parts of my life. Of course, I knew that I reacted to people who were close to me or those who could directly impact my life. But only as I developed this process did I begin to understand that almost all of my feelings were a direct response to relationships with other people. In fact, people I barely knew could affect my whole day.

I came to see relationships as any interaction with another personality that causes emotional, physical, mental, or spiritual responses in us. This definition greatly expands the concept of relationships. It makes us include the man who cuts in front of us in traffic, endangers our safety, and then throws us the one-finger salute. Likewise, if we get upset with the woman who jumps in front of us in line because she sees a friend there, we just developed a relationship with her. We may also have a relationship with that person we completely exclude from our life because he or she did something unacceptable.

Whenever we have an external or internal reaction to another person, we have a relationship with that person. It may be instant and temporary, but it is a relationship. This means that each of us participates in hundreds of relationships. But to get a manageable starting point for understanding relationships, we're going to focus our attention on special relationships, those close associations that are a pivotal part of our lives. After we develop the skills to improve these, we can apply the same principles to other relationships.

Problems versus Symptoms in Relationships

When we have a problem in a relationship, we're faced with a number of different theories about how we should solve it. Many current models for improving relationships ignore any spiritual aspect. Other approaches stress the spiritual component but fail to acknowledge the power of the mind. Many do not recognize the interconnection and dependence of the three basic relationships (spiritual, self, and others), or they fail to recognize the prioritized order in which these must be built. These methods do offer some good practices and concepts. They help some people some of the time, but they often limit their effectiveness because they concentrate on symptoms rather than the real problem.

Our extensive look at the self-relationship revealed that our feelings were the symptom *but the primal problems are impaired integrity, lack of self-love, and self-based decisions.* Only when we solve these basic problems can we hope to alleviate the symptoms.

Breaking the Cycle

The concept of a natural order provides a complementary view of the symptom, problem, and solution in these associations. The distressing symptoms—feelings of misery—emerge and become apparent in relationships with other people; the root problem lies in the self-relationship; and the solution, if it cannot be found and implemented with our mental and physical energies, can always be found in the spiritual relationship.

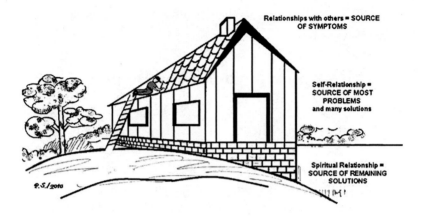

My first attempt using this logical, systematic approach to relationships made me realize that I just did not know *how* to have healthy, rewarding relationships. I wanted to have them; I tackled them with utmost sincerity and desire; I was willing to work on them. But I didn't have the tools that yielded the fulfilling relationships that I craved.

Millions of other people experience this same frustration and disappointment. Most of us want fantastic relationships but we're confused about how to get them. We remain stuck in a cycle of relationship problems. Now, we can apply the same engineering tools to these relationships with other people that we used in our spiritual and self-relationships to eliminate a lot of the confusion and mystery. Using these tools requires that we move out of our current paradigm of relationships to find a new way of understanding these human affiliations, a way that will actually produce the extraordinary results that we want to enjoy.

Developing Relationships with Others: The Solution

"Experience teaches only the teachable."

—Aldous Huxley

I like a clean windshield on my truck. When my windshield gets a blob of dirt on it, my attention immediately concentrates on the black spot. I miss the fact that the windshield is still mostly clean and the spot does not really affect my vision. That spot becomes difficult for me to ignore. I recently noticed that this same attitude carries over into other areas of my life. In some places it seems to help me, but in others, it definitely has the potential to cause problems. If I hear a slight miss in my car's engine, taking care of the small, detectable problem prevents bigger ones that take a lot more time, energy, and money to solve. If insects get in my garden and start destroying my plants, taking care of the problem before they multiply just makes sense. But this clean windshield pattern of response—focusing on the small problems—doesn't extrapolate well to relationships.

My wife, Patricia, and I share an extraordinary, loving relationship. She is a warm, passionate, unselfish, giving person; however, she sometimes does things I don't like. If I'm feeling judgmental, I might even view one of these minor incidents as a mistake. I might even be astounded at how she could say or do such a thing. I've learned that it helps to step back and look at the event in context and not let my spot-on-the-windshield pattern dominate my thinking. If I focus on this single, isolated event, my mind will magnify the small smudge until that's all I see. Then, I'll ignore all the beautiful, wonderful things that she does ninety-nine percent of the time. Having this perception, even for a short time, skews and distorts the reality of the relationship. It can also lead me into reacting and making poor decisions, creating real turmoil out of an insignificant event.

Even if Patricia does make a mistake, it's just a small dark speck on an otherwise beautiful scene. No one is perfect; no relationship can be perfect. None of us will have an absolutely clean panorama. I must appreciate the wonderful blessings and rewards of this love and not be diverted by those isolated, small flecks of gray.

While the windshield pattern doesn't seem to transfer well from technical work to relationships, there are scientific laws that can help us to better understand our relationships.

Physical Laws and Relationships

We can adapt Newton's first law of motion to become the law of motion in relationships. This variation indicates that if we keep doing what we're doing, we'll keep getting what we're getting. If nothing changes, *nothing* changes applies in all our relationships.

Let's say that there's turmoil in one of our relationships. We've tried a number of things to improve the situation with little success. Newton's law would suggest that we examine our attempts and look for a new direction, a new method of action and response that produces different results. For example, we might say, "I've tried what I saw my parents do; I tried what my friends suggested; I read the books and magazines and tried what they advised." Perhaps those focus on the symptom rather than on the problem. Or they may have little hard evidence of achieving successful results. The *something different* we're looking for might include a solution that weeds out the symptoms and offers concrete, proven answers.

Our old enemy *entropy* will deteriorate our relationships, unless we work to overcome its effects. The end product of entropy is not a sudden change but a slow eroding of our commitment, like moving water that slowly wears away a solid rock. It may slide us into habits that do not reflect our true priorities. For example, we may say—and sincerely mean—that our family is important to us, but this must be demonstrated in our actions. Entropy can gradually pull us into patterns that reflect something different. We may spend too much time on the computer at home, start to find another woman or man attractive instead of building our current relationship, watch television for hours instead of playing with our children, or forget to take our wife flowers for no reason other than that we love her.

When it comes to working on our relationships, remember that relationships are built; they don't just happen. Building anything takes energy, and we only have so much energy to give out, so we need to use it efficiently. We need to have a blueprint, the correct tools, and then do the work efficiently, if we want the best results for the least amount of effort.

That Special Relationship

We participate in myriad relationships, but finding and building that intimate, loving relationship, the one with our soul mate, gains the most attention. Here, two key ingredients help determine our success: matching with the right partner, and finding and using a proven process that delivers the results we desire.

Avoiding problems is always easier than solving them. In marriage or a long-term intimate relationship, we enjoy an advantage we don't have in many of our other relationships. We actually get to choose our partner. Making the best choice eliminates a lot of possible problems, but we often start these serious relationships without an objective evaluation. We meet someone and become infatuated. We get stuck on what we want and become afraid of what we might miss. Then cupid's chemistry complicates things even more and we make a less-than-stellar initial bonding choice. Something about the desire for an intimate relationship overrides all of our warning signals. We may overlook obvious core differences that can indicate trouble ahead.

I make no claim to be an expert on how to pick a relationship partner. However, I can offer a few observations, based on my own experience and that of friends, family, and hundreds of people working with the these techniques. As always, mistakes contribute greatly to experience. My three marriages offer some prime examples of what can contribute to the success or failure of a marriage. I've made many mistakes but I have slowly learned how to do a few things right. I have seen many other people get similar results when participating in variations of these three examples.

Immature Relationships

In my first experience, I married my high school sweetheart. We thought we were deeply in love and that this was a forever relationship. In hindsight, I made a lot of mistakes entering this relationship and in trying to make it work.

On the outside, I was a mature, responsible young man. I didn't drink through high school and college; I received a scholarship and worked heavy construction to pay for college; I was never in trouble, and I was a leader in many areas. But my inner life felt quite different. I was emotionally immature, with little idea of my own basic values, and I definitely had an impaired integrity. I had to overachieve to feel worthy. I sought approval and accolades from others. I had no male role models or any idea how to handle my emotions, and I had absolutely no self-confidence in relationships with women.

Finding someone who said she loved me and gave me a little attention was all I needed to make a serious commitment. I was not going to risk giving that up and taking a chance on not finding anyone else who would want me. Had I possessed these simple tools, I may have seen the multitude of indicators screaming that this relationship had little chance of being what we both so desperately wanted:

> Emotional immaturity
> Even prior to our marriage, my first wife and I developed a pattern of fighting for control; we repeatedly disagreed, argued, and hurt each other and then made up, swearing to change and pledging devotion. I gave her power over my feelings, allowing her to push my buttons and make me feel angry, guilty, or fearful.

> Different core values
> We went together for years as teenagers, but we never understood the core differences in our value systems that would emerge as some of our primary problems. The right tools and attitudes can transcend many differences, but basic value differences are difficult to overcome.

> In love with the idea of love
> We knew that we argued and that this association was turbulent, but we had the idealistic belief that love conquered all. However, we had healthy love confused with infatuation and the unhealthy desire to use each other to compensate for our own inadequacies. We had no understanding of what constituted healthy love.

> Unhealthy expectations
> I hoped that the commitment of marriage, of working together, would alleviate our disagreements and turmoil.

It may be hard to conceive that anything good could come out of this relationship that started with such challenges. However, a number of positive things did evolve. Most importantly, we had two beautiful children. They did suffer to some degree from our inadequacies and struggles; however, they managed to mature, and hopefully, they have learned from the errors of their parents. Both of our children have families and careers, and they are relatively happy, but each of them paid a price for our lack of skills.

The marriage was not all doom and gloom. We shared some happy moments, especially with the children. I made many mistakes as a partner and as a parent. Without proper training and a clear process for living and enjoying life, mistakes and consequences were the only way I had to learn. Sometimes I was a slow and stubborn student, so I kept repeating the same mistakes. But even this turned out to have value. My deepest hurts, my abject disappointments, and the most dismal personal failures set the groundwork for growth. If she and I had grown just a little more and reached a point of tolerated stagnation, I might still be mired in accepting mediocrity. My part in this failed marriage was a major driving force that spurred me to find solutions for my problems with feelings and relationships.

We both wanted a good relationship, but we didn't know how to achieve it. We started our union with warning flags sprouting up all over the place, and we had no direction, no process to help us through the maze. Near the end we went to a marriage counselor, but by that time neither of us was willing to listen and try again. This first marriage ended in a disastrous divorce. The children paid the highest price, and I almost ended my life over it.

Good Relationships

My second wife, Barbara, and I got married before I had recovered from my first failure. Not a great idea. I had little remaining integrity. My self-esteem was destroyed and I was again looking for someone to fill my voids. Shortly after our marriage, I started my quest to find out how to be happy and have good relationships. Personal spirituality became the center point of my life. We reared a family, suffered through the death of her daughter, and endured financial problems; we experienced extreme ups and downs over the span of our twenty-one year alliance.

That was the formative period of what later became the *Spiritual Engineering* practices, even though it was a somewhat tumultuous time. Old patterns and ideas still plagued us both, but we wanted a better life. I was searching for answers and adding to the process. As specific tools developed, we adapted them to our individual lives and our relationship. Part of this was a trial-and-error procedure where we kept only the practices that worked for us and for other people who tried them. Our responses, our feelings, and our attitudes gradually improved and we slowly started having better days.

But after nineteen years of marriage, Barb, who had been very healthy, was diagnosed with advanced lung cancer; she was given two years to live. This brought us closer together and made us grasp the spiritual practices even more. Sharing an oncoming death, living through the physical pain and degradation, experiencing the slow disintegration of a once vibrant life, and being able to endure all of that without fear, recrimination, or blame proved the effectiveness of these spiritual tools once again.

There were a number of positive and negative factors that influenced the probable success or failure of our marriage:

Negative Factors

Impaired integrity
   We were both recently divorced and emotionally damaged. Each of us had a huge emptiness inside of us and we looked at each other for help in feeling complete.

Emotional rebound effect

Neither of us had given our self time to heal our emotional wounds before entering into that relationship.

No concrete plan to make the marriage succeed

We had no blueprint to construct a healthy relationship. We thought that it would happen simply because we were committed to making it happen.

Positive Factors

Shared core values

We both placed a high value on honesty, personal responsibility, fairness, and respect for each other. We believed in God and spirituality, but, initially, we didn't place a high priority on these.

Acceptance of responsibility for failure

We accepted that each of us had contributed to the failures of our previous marriages. We discussed what each of us had done wrong, where each of us had failed, where we tried to accept something that was unacceptable to us, and how this compromised our sense of self-worth.

Willingness to grow

Each of us wanted to grow, to improve our self and this new relationship. We knew that we had to change and we were willing to work at it.

Compatibility

We were very compatible on the physical level and somewhat compatible on our spiritual and mental planes. We did exhibit a high tolerance for the slight to medium differences we had in these areas.

We made an impetuous decision by getting married quickly after our divorces. This does not represent a mature and stable approach to such an important venture. But it still worked out.

Four very explicit reasons helped our partnership succeed in spite of the initial negative factors:

1. We discovered a specific and viable process that enabled us to solve problems as they arose in this relationship.
2. Personal spirituality evolved as a core ingredient for growth.
3. The positive factors just cited provided a framework and incentive that led us to actually apply this new process.
4. The tangible results we experienced made us want to continue using the process.

The process, along with directed effort, *built a success out of a potential failure*, teaching me that relationships, like physical events, follow natural laws and logic.

After Barb died, I grieved and I hurt. I tried to move on with life. The hospice counselor who had met with us during the last two weeks before Barb's death told me, "Tom, in the seventeen years I have been a grief counselor, I have only seen one other couple go through this ordeal with the peace and love that you and Barb demonstrated. You should share how you did this with other people." I remembered that I had seen these practical spiritual techniques help many people transform their lives.

At that moment, I committed to sharing these tools with as many people as I could. It gave me something to do that was not selfish and self-centered, and all the time and attention I devoted to others helped me to heal. Practicing these principles repeatedly had finally helped me to accept myself. But I had shared most of my adult life with a woman, and it felt unnatural to be alone. I wanted to look for someone to fill the void inside of me and I started down that path, but the new patterns established in my mind and soul reminded me that this would not be a wise choice. I knew that I had to do more than give these principles lip service, so I worked on my spiritual and self-relationships, spending many hours in prayer and self-examination. I finally reached the point at which I knew at my deepest level of being that I didn't need another person to validate me or make me feel whole. I totally accepted the fact that I could be alone and still have a rich, fulfilling life.

Extraordinary Relationships

Shortly after I knew in my deepest heart that I did not need another partner, I met Patricia, a native of Colombia, at a spiritual retreat. God has an amazing sense of humor and timing. Neither one of us was supposed to be there. I had planned to leave for work overseas, but delay after delay kept pushing ahead my departure date. For Patricia, it was a last-minute decision that brought her to our rendezvous.

We met and immediately started talking. Of course, I noticed her beauty and poise—she's a striking woman. That formed an initial attraction, but our discussion captivated me. We shared our vision of what we wanted to do with our lives, of how we wanted to help people find a better life and find a spiritual relationship that would give them strength and guidance in life.

We parted, not planning to meet again, but we accidentally (?) met a second time at the retreat's final dinner party, just as I was walking out the door to leave. Again, it was like we had known each other forever. With everything we discussed, our agreement on these core values and our compatibility became more and more obvious. We found each other physically attractive, but that just opened the door. Our conversation was immersed in mental challenges and stimulation—an exhilarating experience. We connected with a spiritual bond that I had never experienced before.

As we sat on a porch looking at the beautiful Rocky Mountains a hummingbird came out of nowhere and hovered just three inches in front of Patricia's face. It lingered there for what felt like minutes, but it was probably only twenty to thirty seconds. Then it came to me and flitted just three or four inches in front of my eyes for the longest time; it then returned to Patricia and hovered near her again before it flew away.

We sat in quiet amazement. As a practical engineer, I didn't believe in signs or supernatural forces working to show us something special, but I did think this bird's behavior was a little odd.

As night approached, we moved to a quiet wooded area to talk and watch the moon rise. Midnight came and we continued talking. An inspirational push, coming from somewhere deep inside of me, overshadowed my rational thinking and my rules about making quick decisions. I knew—against all logic—that I wanted to spend the rest of my life with Patricia. I wanted her beside me while I tried to help other people. I distinctly remember telling her, "We will be together for the rest of our lives." She looked directly into my eyes and replied, "Yes, Thomas, we will."

I had briefly described the principles of the *Spiritual Engineering* process to Patricia, and I told her that, if this relationship worked out, she would always be third in my life. I said I hoped that she would hold me in the same priority. My relationship with God had to stay in first place. I had to maintain my integrity and self-respect, but she would be the most important person on this planet to me and I would show that in my words and actions. We agreed to build our relationship with these practical tools.

We didn't run out and get married; we slowly developed and nurtured our relationship. We shared our dreams, goals, values, ideals, and experiences. We played and laughed. We prayed. We knew that we wouldn't always agree so we made an early pact that we will always be loving toward one another. We started our very first morning together with prayer and meditation. In the beginning there were some hurt feelings and emotional turmoil. We started pausing and asking for guidance, separately and as a couple, before the contention got out of hand. We continued our attempt to build and reinforce healthy patterns. As a result, our bond strengthened, yielding an extraordinary union that's beyond our wildest dreams.

Before our partnership formed, we had no idea of how much happiness, joy, and love two people could experience from sharing core values, a vision to help humanity, a willingness to grow and working a process based on the Natural Order of Relationships. At this point in our lives, our relationship reinforces the value and credibility of the these tools. Many couples using this model have experienced similar results.

Start Right and Have a Process

Variations of these three examples from my life probably fit a lot of relationships, and they demonstrate some critical indicators of the likelihood of a successful relationship. First of all, relationships must be built; they don't just happen. They require commitment, direction, and effort. Erecting them with a specific and proven blueprint provides the best chance of experiencing the highest quality relationship. The intimate partnership that we desire with another person does not exist in isolation. It forms as the pinnacle of all our human relationships. The more it rests on a solid foundation and supporting structure, the better the chances that it will fulfill the potential of both partners.

However, if we wait until we have complete integrity and a perfect spiritual relationship, we'll never get into a relationship in this lifetime. We usually enter into these intimate partnerships while we're striving for growth. That's just the way it is, but this process has laid some groundwork to help us logically evaluate which traits and attitudes are important, so we will have the best chance of being happy, joyous, and loving.

We can summarize this in a few ideas that increase our likelihood to enjoy an extraordinary relationship Both partners should:

1. share similar core values
2. exhibit a degree of physical, mental, spiritual, and emotional compatibility
3. have loving tolerance and respect for differences
4. have, or be willing to jointly find, a proven process that
   a. builds the relationship on a natural order
   b. establishes the nature and priority of the three primal relationships
   c. helps each person grow individually
   d. builds and nurtures the union
5. actively and continuously work on that process
6. commit to the idea that being happy is more important than being right, never hesitate to admit mistakes, and demonstrate healthy forgiveness.
7. exhibit the desire to share their great fortune with others.

All of these steps are essential. Sharing core values and having a high degree of compatibility might seem to be all that is needed for "finding our soul mate." Although they're very important, they're not enough by themselves to insure the best union. Remember that almost fifty million people have experienced divorce in this country. Even random odds make it likely that many of these couples, perhaps millions, had what they considered to be a soul mate. Nonetheless, they still failed because they did not have effective techniques to fulfill the relationship's potential.

Knowing and understanding our own core values, personality traits, and attitudes toward our physical, mental, and spiritual life arenas are not things that we generally sit around and think about. Today we have a lot of help. Personality tests with competent interpretation can greatly augment our tolerance and understanding of each other and of our self. As many of these emphasize, we can learn to appreciate, instead of denigrate, the differences that always exist between individuals. Some dating companies even offer these tests as part of their services. However, it's one step on a long journey. Each relationship must be built, and having effective tools to construct the union is absolutely necessary to share an extraordinary experience.

Interestingly, many seeming hurdles are easily overcome. Patricia and I have merged her Latin culture and my rural American background with very few upsets. Differences in outlook on family, politics, church attendance, historical influences on our attitudes, music, hobbies, and other points have not only melted, but they have provided a source of appreciation for each other's viewpoints and values.

Developing Relationships with Others: Implementing the Solution

"The meeting of two personalities is like the contact of two chemical substances: if there is any reaction, both are transformed."

—Carl Jung

Even for a practical engineer, feelings determine much of the quality of my life, and relationships bring out some of my best and worst feelings. My intimate partnerships have taken me from near suicide to the heights of joy, love, devotion, compassion, understanding, and exhilaration over sharing experiences with a soul mate. For many years when it came to relationships and feelings, I was just along for the ride. I reacted, with little control, and I had no way to solve the problems I encountered.

These logical tools changed that for me, as they have for many others. They offer solutions that actually produce results. Of course, we cannot change the established habits of a lifetime overnight. In any relationship, we must stop giving other people power over our emotions and remember that whenever we choose to volunteer for misery, we are making a mistake. No law or ethical code forces us to automatically accept misery from others or our selves. We have a choice, but learning to make that choice requires practice and discipline.

Practice

Patricia and I committed to these principles from the first night we met, and I've been striving to practice them for years, but it's sometimes difficult to remember them in the midst of a busy life.

Many of our problems start, or become exacerbated, in our mind, so we take proactive measures to keep our mental giants under control. We read daily spiritual thoughts, share prayers, and meditate together, following the same guidelines discussed in this book. We try to support and help each other stay centered in this new model for relationships, always striving to appreciate the wonderful differences between us and demonstrate love and respect for each other.

Of course, we're human and we make mistakes; we still have our old patterns vying for control because each of us has personal areas that need improvement. We have disagreements and contention, but we know that the process will work when we use it. We avoid major conflicts by pausing and getting back to the natural order before things get too intense. This is much more effective when we can do it at the start of a contention rather than waiting until it gets more emotionally powerful.

After we had been together for a year, we had a little ceremony in which we formally invited God, as each us understood him to join us as the managing partner of this relationship. (We still don't agree on all of the details of the spiritual life, but that's quite all right.) We did that to help increase our conscious awareness that our individual and joint spiritual relationships are the foundation of our union.

Now, when we find symptoms of misery overtaking us, or when we're faced with an imminent disagreement, Patricia has invoked a truly beneficial technique. We sit down and ask our spiritual manager to join in the discussion, and we pull out a chair for him to sit and join in. We actually have a chair at our kitchen table labeled the "God's chair" to remind us of the spiritual aspect of our discussions.

Then we actively and audibly include this third party in our talk. Let me tell you, it is much more difficult to be angry and to say hurtful or selfish things when you are consciously aware that God, or your spiritual leader, is sitting there aware of everything—especially when your partner says something like, "Okay, Father, listen to what my husband has to say about this situation and how he talks to your daughter." That changes the whole tone and direction of the conversation.

I still have a problem, at times, with anger and self-righteousness flaring up and interfering with my peace of mind. When I start to get a little angry, my mind justifies this feeling and reinforces my unwillingness to change. I mentally and emotionally dig in my heels, as if to say, "I'm justified in feeling this way. Just leave me alone and let me suffer." These feelings may last a few minutes or a few hours; it all depends on what action I take to alleviate them.

I don't like to volunteer for misery or let it dominate my life anymore. I use everything I can to avoid negative, draining feelings or to move out of them quickly. For example, one time after getting into this mood over some trivial matter, I made an "Attitude Adjustment Coupon" that I presented to Patricia. I originally did this as a joke, but it has proven so beneficial that she still uses it. It has been a great tool to move me back toward the natural order and help restore my mental peace and equilibrium.

Now, we both carry one of these cards, and we've passed them on to hundreds of people. The coupon itself best explains how it works.

Attitude Adjustment Coupon

The undersigned person recognizes that he may temporarily act in a manner that is not loving, kind, or caring. He acknowledges that there may be brief intervals when his thinking and reactions may be *slightly* wrong. To minimize the turmoil caused by this rare condition, this coupon gives the bearer the right to require that the undersigned person:

1. Pause, remain quiet for five minutes, and try to pray
2. Seriously consider the very slim possibility that he might be wrong
3. Think about how much the bearer of this coupon demonstrates her love for him.

Following this, both parties agree to share a prayer and then start the conversation with "I love you because…" and state three reasons why they love the other person.

To insure compliance with this request, if I do not immediately complete the above actions, I agree to be the total slave of the bearer of this coupon for one full week.

This coupon is valid for eternity and is automatically renewed with each use.

_____ Signature

(Note: This coupon is available on the spiritual-engineering.com website)

Healthy Love

Of course, the admonition to "Love your neighbor as yourself" is the key to all great relationships. It's that simple. In this discussion, love has a specific meaning: to demonstrate an active, healthy concern for another person, which implies that we have to learn to love with wisdom. There are a few attributes that distinguish healthy love such as discernment, congruency, honesty, and enlightened forgiveness.

Spiritual Engineering Axiom #9

Love with wisdom

Discernment

Discernment is an important attribute that helps to distinguish between mistakes and patterns. In any relationship, each partner will make mistakes. If someone makes a mistake or does something with which we disagree, that often becomes the spot on the windshield. We shouldn't give a lot of attention to the small stuff.

Patterns are a different matter.

Say our partner takes the money we need for our mortgage and wastes it gambling, shopping, or drinking. He promises to quit but doesn't live up to the promise. Or he's abusive over and over again after promising that he will stop. These are patterns. Specifically, these are negative patterns of *repeatedly making the same mistake after committing to change*. Some of these may reflect the disease of addiction, others may be bad habits, and still others may just be irresponsible and immature behavior. It's important to distinguish between mistakes and patterns so we can decide on an appropriate response. Occasional mistakes, even bad mistakes, have hope for change; patterns are very difficult to change. Love and tolerance may lead us to accept some patterns, but others may prove unacceptable.

The *Spiritual Engineering* process recognizes the difficulty of changing entrenched behaviors. It outlines definite factors that are required for long-lasting change.

Five Factors Required for Change

We must

1. Accept the problem.
2. Want to solve the problem.
3. Identify a solution that works.
4. Implement this solution–do the work.
5. Perform the necessary maintenance.

All of these factors must be in place before any long-lasting change will take effect. They apply to anyone who wants change, whether it's our self or someone else. They also clarify why we cannot make another person change. We can lead, browbeat, threaten, and coerce, but we can rarely instill the acceptance or the basic desire for change. That has to be self-initiated.

Congruency

Congruency teaches us to help—but not enable—other people. We can help them without interfering with their growth, their freewill choice, or the consequences of those choices. This moves the responsibility of helping others to a different level. We cannot act indiscriminately; we must take responsibility for examining the situation. We must make certain that our action actually helps and doesn't harm that person. We look at our perceptions, our expectations, and our motives.

Here, we examine *how* we are evaluating the situation, *what* we expect from the other person (and our self) if we perform this act, and *why* we are going to do what we propose to do. For example, we can ask ourselves: Do I have any selfish motives? Am I trying to make myself feel better? We try to determine how the person got into this position. Was it an accident, a misfortune of nature that brought disease and suffering? Or was it a choice and action on their part that brought about the problem? Is this a one-time occurrence—a mistake—or is it a pattern in the person's life? A pattern will keep repeating itself unless the Five Factors for Change are present.

Acquiring congruency does not come easy. It sometimes goes against what we want to do. When one of my children succumbed to chemical addiction, I wanted to solve the problem, to protect and shield her. I had to learn that my loving, seemingly helpful actions could delay her progress in finding her own solution, and that going through the misery that resulted from her decisions and actions could be an essential part of her journey to recovery. I had to learn that helping included avoiding judgment or recrimination and always being there to support her. Helping did not automatically include taking care of the consequences of her actions. In facing the repercussions of her actions, I could help her accept responsibility and find solutions for them, but I could not do it for her.

Honesty

A key part of honesty includes understanding the seldom-realized difference between truth and fact. Truth relates to the spiritual life arena, facts to the physical and/or mental life arenas. Sharing the truth embodies mature love, an active, healthy concern for a person's well-being. Telling facts may have nothing to do with this. Truth builds and enhances both the giver and receiver. Depending on the wisdom with which they are used, facts can help *or* harm people. As the examples below demonstrate, truth involves examining our perceptions, motives, and the receptivity of the receiver. Facts are impartial physical evidence; they just simply are. Facts exist exactly as they are no matter what our opinion or motivation. This distinction may seem too subtle or frivolous, but is quite important for building healthy, loving relationships. Let's look at some examples to clarify this point.

If my six-year-old daughter asks me where babies come from, what do I tell her? If I tell her all the *facts* about conception, childbirth, and labor, I may risk psychologically harming this young child. She may not be ready to receive and process this information. As the older, wiser parent, I must select my facts carefully and give them to the child as she matures and becomes ready to receive them. I don't deny or hide the facts; I use them to impart truth at each stage of her development.

In a very different example, suppose I am driving by a motel and I see a friend's wife emerging from the motel with another man. Do I tell my friend or anyone else about what I saw? What is my motive for saying anything at all? What if they were attending a conference or meeting that I knew nothing about? What if they were having lunch to plan a surprise birthday party for him? Do I hide a slightly sinister motive behind the cloak of "Well, he should know about this; I need to protect him"? If I decide to tell anyone, am I doing it to build myself up, to show that I know something that someone else doesn't?

This distinction between truth and fact destroys all justification for gossip. This insidious evil is often justified with the rationalizing thought, "Well, it's okay to say this; I'm just telling the truth." But gossip, while it may be factual, can seldom be truthful. It cannot pass the tests of mature love or spiritual motivation. This view also includes the one who is listening. Listening to gossip makes me as responsible as the teller. Can my listening ever be a truly loving and well-motivated act? Listening makes me participate in a non-truth. Without a listener, the gossip dies.

Enlightened Forgiveness

How often have we heard the admonition to "forgive and forget"? However, this new pragmatic way to engage in this spiritual life teaches us to forgive but never forget. That is quite a difference.

When someone does us a real or imagined wrong, we *must* forgive that person if we are to achieve integrity and peace within our self. However, forgetting what happened—wiping the event, the circumstances surrounding that event, and the other person's contribution to these from our memory—will make us susceptible to repeating that hurt. Therefore, we must totally let go of the *feeling* associated with the event but retain the factual memory of what happened.

Harboring resentment, guilt, or blame prevents us from being loving, and it blocks our own growth. On the other hand, we also realize that our progressive maturity, our developing wisdom, is partially based on learning from our actions and our responses to other people's actions. If we forget everything, we lose the opportunity to learn from our experience. We must release the feeling but retain the experience.

Spiritual Engineering—with its integrated Natural Order of Relationships, problem-solving techniques, and focus on personal responsibility—removes some of the mystery from relationships. Applying these logical, practical, and systematic tools provides an opportunity to experience some of the very best relationships and emotions possible. The same process helps us minimize our volunteering for misery and gives us some specific guidelines for dealing with the emotional pain that is an unavoidable part of all of our lives.

PART FIVE

The Lifelong Challenge of Overcoming Ingrained Patterns and Entropy

Life Gives Us Pain: Loving Makes Us Vulnerable

"He who has felt the deepest grief is best able to experience supreme happiness. We must have felt what it is to die, that we may appreciate the enjoyments of life."

—Alexander Dumas

It wasn't a late-night call that brought the tragic news. The call came at two in the afternoon when I was home alone. My stepdaughter had been terribly injured in a car accident. The state police could only tell me where and when the accident occurred and that they were immediately moving her to a hospital. I managed to glean a few details: she was in a car that had been rear-ended by a bus; she was not wearing a seat belt, and she had been thrown through the windshield.

Such a call is a parent's most dreaded nightmare.

I sat at the kitchen table to catch my breath. My stepdaughter Michelle and I had an extremely close bond. We were alike in so many ways. This news felt like acid inside, eating holes in me and spreading pain. I knew that it would devastate her mother. Barb was at work that day so I went there to tell her. We rushed home and arranged for neighbors to watch our two small children.

I tried to handle the details, get directions to the hospital, get money from the bank, make sure that the other children had what they needed, and comfort Barb. I again called the state police.

Instead of taking Michelle to Rock Springs, Wyoming, they were Life Flighting her to a Salt Lake City trauma unit because of her severe head injuries. She was still alive, but her injuries were definitely life-threatening.

We set out on our four-hour drive to the hospital. Fear and apprehension dominated every second of our trip. There were no cell phones at that time, so we kept wondering if Michelle was still alive, and if she lived, what her condition and quality of life would be. My children had given me moments of gut-wrenching fear before, but this one stretched beyond limits and made it nearly impossible to drive.

Barb and I reviewed the chain of events that had set this tragedy in motion. We had known for some time that Michelle was living with her boyfriend. She had recently told us that he had a drug problem and that they argued, sometimes violently. She refused to leave him. She wanted to stay with him and get him into a recovery program, but he was unwilling to go. Michelle, Barb, and I had talked about all this just the week before. We tried to talk her into coming home. We tried to tell her that no one can be forced to accept help, that she may be putting herself in danger if she stayed. But we faced the same situation with her that she faced with her boyfriend: We couldn't make her do what was obviously best for her. She was nineteen and very independent.

When we got to the hospital, the staff told us that Michelle had died on the way to the trauma unit.

Sometimes Life Hurts

Loving others makes us vulnerable to pain. People disappoint us—they leave us, they betray us, and sometimes they die. Bad things happen to everyone. Emotional pain is inevitable, but misery is optional. We can develop skills to help eliminate or minimize the misery in our lives, but nothing can teach us how to avoid the pain that will hit us in a lifetime. If we love other people, we are going to feel pain.

Pain includes grief, sadness, and some forms of guilt, shame, disappointment, loneliness, and discouragement. Experiencing pain not only hurts—it renders us more susceptible to misery. It's like an open wound that's vulnerable to infection. However, there are steps we can take to prevent this contamination. Misery is preventable. When overwhelming emotions hit, we can determine whether they are pain or misery, and then we can apply the appropriate tools.

The next chapter offers tools to minimize or eliminate misery; but right now, let's look at what we can do to facilitate healing when emotional pain tears us apart.

Inevitable Emotional Pain

Let's start with one of the hardest events any of us will face: the death of a loved one.

When death or separation ends a profound love, how does the surviving person move on with their life? What enables one person to work through grief while another lives in misery for years? Unhealthy mourning may indicate heartfelt loss or it may simply demonstrate a lack of adequate tools to process the grief. Some people become mired in sadness and despair, and their yearning for a lost love may go on for years, which can devastate their lives and cripple relationships with family and friends. Others try to simply ignore the pain and move on, but we cannot just lay that kind of pain aside. Grief can be processed in a healthy, effective way.

Like so many things in life, I've learned about healthy grieving through experience. I've grieved the death of three brothers, four sisters, my mother, my stepdaughter Michelle, my second wife, and close friends. I've made mistakes that have increased my misery over these losses, but I have also learned things that have helped me move through the losses. Again, answers lie in a universal order, starting with the Natural Order of Relationships.

Grief and the Spiritual Relationship

Thoughts of the person you lost will naturally dominate your thinking after the loss, but do not neglect the foundation of all relationships. An enlightened understanding offers valuable help during a period of grief.

When Barbara and I lost Michelle, our spiritual understanding formed the bedrock for our healing. It did not eliminate the horrible sense of loss, the anguish that ripped our hearts and souls, the thoughts of the wedding, births, grandchildren, and everything else that we would miss sharing with her. Our beliefs didn't prevent sleepless nights or waking up at three in the morning when I had finally fallen off to sleep only an hour before, but it gave me something to turn to that eased some of my pain. My spiritual life became a refuge, a haven where I could find comfort and security.

I didn't blame God for this accident. God didn't build the car, the highway, or the vehicles. People had done that. People had also made mistakes that led to the tragedy. I didn't have to try to understand how God could let it happen; I already held a pretty firm belief about the power of freewill choice. I knew that he would not interfere with that gift. People made wrong decisions, things happened, and other people got hurt. That's just the way life—and death—often work.

Some of our core spiritual beliefs proved to be invaluable. For your consideration, here are a few concepts that provided comfort for us, and they have since helped many others as well:

- God does not *take* people; He *receives* them.
- God does not cause pain; He alleviates misery.
- He does not give us tests; He provides solutions.
- Death is an interruption, not the end, of a relationship. It's a comma, not a period.
- Someone else's freewill choice can cause pain in my life.

Years later, these ideals again proved their worth when Barbara fought her battle with cancer. We had shared a loving nineteen-year relationship when she was diagnosed with lung cancer. Not once did we wonder why God allowed this to happen or believe that he visited this affliction upon her. Her doctor had warned her that smoking while taking a certain prescription that significantly increased her risk of cancer. She continued in spite of that. She couldn't break the addiction, and she accepted responsibility for her choices and actions.

Part of her treatment included chemotherapy with its ensuing weakness, vomiting, and reduction of human dignity. I still remember the day her hair came out in handfuls in the shower. She lost over half of her beautiful blond hair in only one day, and the rest fell out shortly after. We cried and held each other. With many facets of this disease and treatment, I was able to be there for support, but she was the one who experienced the full pain. Later that week she was trying on wigs and scarves and laughing again.

Cancer and chemotherapy strip away our vanity and get to matters that are more important—life, death, and the constant choice of whether we wring what happiness we can from each moment or wallow in self-pity, recrimination, and fear. Barb and I knew that our minds dictated our emotional responses to every event and that this situation made us extremely vulnerable to negative responses. We needed guidance and power to avoid these pitfalls. We adamantly practiced the daily exercises and used every tool we had to keep fear from corroding our minds.

Just before Christmas, after fourteen months of treatment, Barb was declared cancer-free. Our family celebrated the holidays and anticipated a new year without the constant burden of physical degradation and impending death. But a checkup three months later delivered a different verdict. The cancer had returned with a vengeance. A few cells must have remained hidden, and they had silently spread across the lungs and metastasized to the liver.

Cancer spread within her body like wildfire in a dry wind. The doctors gave Barb only months to live.

Our remaining time together was a dichotomy of emotion. We accepted the fact of her oncoming death and we vowed to enjoy our remaining time as much as possible. From experience, we knew that living according to these principles would yield power and real results. We didn't expect a miraculous healing, but we had complete confidence that our spiritual relationship, along with actively using the practical tools, would give us the best possible way to endure that experience.

Over the next few months, I watched life leave Barb as she deteriorated rapidly. I stayed home and nursed her during the final weeks. Even when we knew that death was only days away, we found some sparks of joy and laughter. Sitting beside the bed, wiping her brow with a damp cloth, giving her sips of water, I shared her final moments with love and unseen tears.

Life hurts sometimes, and it helps to have answers that work when we have to go through that pain.

Grief and the Self-Relationship

When we lose someone we love, a part of us is *really gone*. The hole in our heart is real. In that vulnerable state, we must make careful, conscious choices about filling the emptiness. It's not unusual to experience a range of feelings, thoughts, and physical reactions. All of these may hit within a short period of time. For example:

- Our emotional state may range from total numbness to very intense emotions and rapid mood changes. We may be angry with others, or with God. We may feel guilt or remorse over something we said or did. Despair and hopelessness may dominate us.
- Our mental state may be as confused as our emotions. Concentration may be fragmented; we may notice lapses in memory. It may be difficult to complete simple tasks,

such as paying our bills. Our thoughts may wander without a specific direction. We may ask ourselves: "How am I going to survive without him or her? What am I going to do?" or, "Why did this have to happen?"

- Physical reactions may include difficulty in sleeping and eating, or anxiety attacks. We may feel exhausted at times and full of energy at others. We may feel acceptance and peace one minute and then suddenly break into tears for no apparent reason.

We will react in different ways. Each of us may experience some of these examples, none of them, or something totally different. Our responses occur in the spiritual, mental, and physical life arenas. Those three arenas also provide *three separate and distinct sources of energy* to help us transcend the pain of grief and avoid misery. Again, common sense tells us that utilizing three complementing power sources will solve any problem more efficiently than using only one or two.

In the spiritual life arena, a practical spiritual life does not claim miracle cures or deliverance from all adversity. It can lead to better decisions that help avoid many problems; however, it's an inescapable fact that nature, accidents, and mis-guided free will choices may sometimes cause pain. This way of life offers us a choice of how we will move through it. You can develop skills to help you endure such hardships with dignity, freedom from fear, and the ability to wring the last drop of joy and happiness possible from moment-by-moment experiences. Blaming God for those kinds of events moves us out of the natural order and separates us from a powerful resource that can help transcend this pain. Even if we don't believe in God, or if we believe that God caused the problem, this innovative method stresses that *action* opens the channel to every person's inner spiritual power. Once it's accessed, this energy inevitably responds if we sincerely want relief from our devastating emotional pain. The results will come if we remain open-minded and take action.

When you're bogged down in pain, it's helpful to review the spiritual exercises. Recommit to spending fifteen to twenty minutes each day to transform your life. Knowing that results depend on action might lead us to actually *do* the morning, daytime, and nighttime exercises. Establish communication with your inner guide. Spend extra time in strengthening this relationship.

When an unavoidable personal disaster hits, our mind provides the key to whether we experience healthy grieving or succumb to misery. Disciplining our mind is often more difficult in the throes of deep emotional pain. Try to become more aware of the unconscious decisions that augment your grief, of those old patterns that slide you into self-pity, guilt, or fear. One practical way to shift your thinking is to listen to or read spiritually uplifting material that guides your mind into favorable channels. Try to keep your thoughts in today. This can be more difficult during grief. When your thoughts start dragging you down, pause and ask your inner source to help you focus on what is happening today, on what you can act on right now.

Your physical life arena can also contribute to healing. This arena contains the physical actions you take plus anything concerning your material domain. The physical act of writing about your inner thoughts and feelings often helps. If deep remorse plagues you, if you keep thinking about something that you should have said or done, try writing a sincere letter to the person you've lost. Express your regrets, desires, and wishes. Then read the letter aloud to God and ask that he accept this on behalf of your loved one. Finally, destroy the letter and leave the remorse and regret behind.

Talk to a friend. Share your pain or misery. Sometimes we tend to isolate and hold our emotions in check; we become stoic and we try to bear up under the burden. Sharing grief decreases our pain just as sharing a pie lessens the amount of pie that remains in the dish. Each piece we share eliminates a sliver of grief.

Writing a gratitude list can often shift your attitude. Although you may not feel grateful right now, you can search for people or events for which you are grateful. Try looking for things you take for granted, things that, if they were removed, you would sorely miss. Becoming aware of their value can help make you grateful that you have them. For example:

> If you can see, be grateful.
> If you can hear, be grateful.
> If you can walk, be grateful.
> If you can read, be grateful.
> If you slept in a bed last night, be grateful.
> If you ate today, be grateful.
> If any person cares for you, be grateful.
> If you care for any person, be grateful.

If you have read this far, you are alive, breathing, and able to experience a better day. You are a child of a loving, compassionate divine parent who wants only the best for you. Be grateful.

Sometimes I don't realize the value of things until I lose them. I never truly appreciated the simple gift of sight until I lost my vision, the freedom of movement until I was confined to bed, the ability to walk naturally until I could not move without crutches, or the value of certain relationships until I lost them. Right here, right now, in this very moment, I can find many things for which to be grateful.

In our grief, we may experience times when thoughts and emotions start to overwhelm us and we can't even pray. Sometimes, taking a physical action can get us back on course. We might take a walk to see something different. As we do this, we force our mind and senses to become aware of many beautiful things, like flowers, a child playing, or the shapes of the clouds.

Consider getting a pet. A puppy, or a kitten, gives unconditional love and directs time and attention to something positive. Having a young dog or cat presents opportunities to take physical actions that can change your thinking. Time spent playing with, walking, or training a pet will shift your thoughts away from your problems. Watching them frolic, run, and simply enjoy life can lift your spirits when other things fail.

Many people find that actively helping someone else eliminates some of their own despair and misery. Volunteering at a hospital or soup kitchen changes our environment, gets us out of the house, and directs our thoughts toward helping others.

Don't be afraid to cry, alone or with trusted family or friends. Don't feel embarrassed if you break down and start crying in public or at work. This is your life and your pain. You can't spend time wondering if what you're doing meets the approval of others.

Grief and Relationships with Others

Thoughts of the relationship that was interrupted by death may dominate many of your waking hours. Sadness, loneliness, and mourning are part of healthy grieving. Practical things may require your attention. Handling funeral arrangements or disposing of personal effects can seem like monumental tasks. Handle those as needed, but it's essential that you take care of yourself at this crucial time. Ask family and friends to help. Don't be a martyr.

Consider what you would want the other person to do if the situation were reversed. What if your loved one had survived you? How would you want him or her to handle things? Wouldn't you want the best for that person? Would you want them to extend their grief into years of isolation and misery? Would you want them to grieve your death so much that their relationships with others became impaired? Anyone who loves you would want the same good things for you as you would have for them.

Affirm relationships with friends and family, but be aware that many people do not know how to grieve or to help someone who is grieving. They don't know what to say, or they may say something inappropriate; they may ignore you and not call or visit; they may feel uncomfortable; they may want to help but have no idea what to do. Try to be patient with them.

You may not want to be with other people for a while, but be careful of this. There is a balance. Some time alone, quietly reflecting and meditating, may be helpful; however, too much isolation can lead to despair and depression. As you start to heal, look for opportunities to build new relationships and to be of service to others.

Losses in Living Relationships

Grief also occurs when we lose someone due to divorce, separation, or alienation. The person is living, but the relationship is severed and the sense of loss is acute. We may hope that the loss is temporary, that we might get this relationship back in the future. Or we may accept that the loss is permanent. If so, we may be glad that it is over, *or* we may feel like we have little left to live for.

The natural order doesn't change, whether the loss is due to death or a living loss. Our need for a strong spiritual relationship still forms the foundation for healing. However, a living loss may foster additional symptoms.

You may:

- feel a sense of failure, that you may never have a healthy relationship
- feel jealous, betrayed, angry, and resentful
- feel severe loneliness and sadness

If you initiated the separation, you may:

- deny that this split is important
- second-guess your decision
- worry about other people's opinions

- wish that this person loved you as much as you love him or her
- wish that both of you had been more willing to compromise
- experience the *if* and *if only* syndrome: *If I had done this differently...* or *"If only he or she had or hadn't done those things...*

If the other person terminated the relationship, you may also:

- feel that the separation was not fair or not handled correctly
- feel that you were misled or deceived
- wonder what you could have done differently
- yearn for a reconciliation

These feelings may wash over you and engulf you like a tidal wave. They may dominate your consciousness to the point that you can't think of anything else. They may cause your chest to feel so tight that it seems like you can't breathe. At times like that, it seems impossible for peaceful, loving thoughts to penetrate your confusion and pain. These feelings can form a breeding ground for misery.

Navigating through grief without succumbing to these counterproductive feelings requires discipline and practice. Stay vigilant for the onset of misery. Apply the techniques discussed above to avoid sinking lower. Accept that you are responsible for your feelings. Blaming other people for the way you feel leaves little hope that you will ever feel better. Remember, making others responsible for the problem inherently makes them responsible for the solution, which means that you cannot feel better until *they* change.

Share your pain with trusted friends and family. You don't have to tell all the details of the separation to everyone, but you don't want to isolate yourself either. True friends can be a tremendous help, simply because they care about you and want the best for you. Find a few that you can call at night when these emotions seem to be the worst. When powerful emotions hit late at night, pick up that thousand-pound phone and call them. Talk about how you feel. Most people will feel so honored by your trust in them that they will be glad to talk and listen.

Losing a loved one to death or separation is something we all have to face. Pain is inevitable, but misery is optional. As with most things in life, thinking or wishing accomplishes nothing without action.

Misery Is Optional and Self-Inflicted: It's All about Your Thinking

"I am more and more convinced that our happiness or our unhappiness depends far more on the way we meet the events of life than on the nature of those events themselves."

—Karl Wilhelm von Humboldt

All right. Life is good. You've worked through the process and are living according to the natural order. You feel fine and you think this new way of life is awesome. You're on emotional cruise control when suddenly anger, guilt, worry, or another symptom of misery rears its ugly head. You find yourself immersed in the old emotions, and you wonder, "What happened? I thought I had the answers. What's wrong?"

You do have the answers, but even the best solution on the planet will not overcome the laws of nature and the grasp of lifelong patterns. Our basic humanity will move us to rest on our laurels and take our new peace and joy for granted. Entropy will make sure that we pay a price when we do. This is a journey of continual challenge and progress.

Learning how to live this new way of life requires practice, just as getting better at anything takes practice. Even professional athletes continue to practice. After years of learning and honing their skills in high school, college, and professional sports, they still practice. Like the athlete, we don't have to relearn what we already know; we simply have to continue to learn how to apply it in different situations until it becomes second nature.

As in any other area of life, what we know counts much less than what we do.

When misery returns and disturbs our life, an inner voice may tell us that we're failing, that what we're doing isn't working. Don't listen to it. Everyone experiences falling short of doing what they *think* they should do. This is a natural part of the growth process. Don't get discouraged by temporary shortfalls. Our consistent performance will always be less than our goals. The intervening gap between the two provides the space for growth. We must focus on how far we've come, not on how far we think we have to go.

By now we, hopefully, understand that this current feeling of misery is a symptom and not the real problem, and that such disturbances are usually self-inflicted. We've likely deviated from one of the natural orders. We have either allowed one of the three basic relationships to get out of its order of priority, or we have made choices that prevent unifying our personality. But now we have a choice. We can either stay in misery or get out. We just need to follow the process and take action.

Practice, Practice, Practice

Most of us want a quick fix for problems. Believe it or not, after we've completed the initial work and have experienced results, this practical spiritual approach can offer rapid results. At the first onset of misery, practice the short exercise for "During the Day." Identify the specific feeling. Don't blame, justify, or deny it. Name it and claim it. Then, pause and connect with your inherent source of energy.

Once this practice alleviates turmoil, acknowledge that and give thanks to your spiritual companion for the help. This is important. It reinforces the correlation between asking for help and finding relief, both physically and psychologically. This cause-and-effect association—you need help, you ask for spiritual help, and you get results—establish a new and healthy inner pattern that becomes a cornerstone in your life. This process can move you to peace and happiness when your mind and determination fail.

Still, all of us will have times when pausing and praying doesn't melt away the misery. Sometimes the thought-emotion reaction may develop into a firestorm before we can pause. We quickly pass from feeling peaceful into extreme misery. This occurs less often as we practice the daily exercises, but it may never disappear completely. When it does happen, we need to, again, review the status of our natural orders.

The Natural Orders and Emotional Relapse: The Self-Relationship

Recognize the differences in the symptom, the problem, and the solution. When we experience feelings of misery, the symptom often appears in our relationship with others; the problem is generally in the self-relationship; and the solution will be found in either this relationship or in the spiritual connection. So when we experience those feelings of misery that require a little more effort to expel, we almost certainly need to focus on our self-relationship.

We can start by reviewing our integrity. Why does this issue disturb us so much? What expectations, perceptions, and motives are involved? Are they healthy? How important is it really? Does this involve a situation we want to control? An object we want to possess? Something we want to happen? Has something we *want* become too important? If this involves something we want or don't want, we need to take a closer look at it. Desire can be a positive or negative force. It can push us toward achieving healthy goals and finding fulfillment, or it can drive us to making unhealthy compromises. Does this current desire disturb our peace of mind? Is it in line with our core values and beliefs? Has it become obsessive? What motive prompted this urge?

When misery overtakes us and we can't shake it by taking the initial steps, we may need to make a little more intensive effort. We can start by looking at the underlying source (and sometimes the solution) to many problems: our mind.

The Mental Life Arena and Misery: Think Your Way into Right Acting

We cannot have a problem without having thought about it. Understanding the basic connection between what we think and what we feel is a vital step in alleviating misery. Our feelings follow our thoughts like thunder follows lightning, except that the time delay between thought and feeling sometimes makes the association a little more difficult to observe. Some thoughts precede our misery and other thoughts can lead us out of it.

The process starts when we use our mind to make a decision. We must *choose* whether we want to stay in this feeling or do the work to find a healthier emotional state. Once we decide we want to feel better, we try to become aware of our thoughts and discern whether they are helping us or hurting us. Almost every single thought we have contributes to moving us in one direction or the other; either we stay immersed in the problem or we move toward a solution. There is no in-between. Everything we think, say, or do pushes us deeper into the problem or moves us toward an answer.

In addition to becoming aware of our thoughts, we try to become more aware of our ongoing decisions. Our old patterns likely included making *unconscious self-willed* decisions that automatically kept us immersed in the problem. For example, most of us have probably found ourselves wrapped up in worry at some point without being aware that the choices we were making led us into the worry. Instead, it just seemed to happen. Now, as we use these new tools, we'll progressively move our decisions to the level of *conscious* choices. We'll become aware of making more conscious choices, and we'll be able to see how each of these impacts our feelings.

Be forewarned: Your self-directed mind will probably try to reassert its authority for a long time. It's the spoiled child that got its way most of your life and it does not want to change. Adding to this challenge, the entrenchment of these old patterns may involve more than just retraining your mind. One current theory postulates that our bodies become addicted to the chemicals that are produced when we experience strong emotions. At a basic cellular level, our internal mechanisms develop a need for those exact chemicals. Repeating old patterns over and over creates an ingrained emotional/chemical release/physical response pattern. Our body begins to unconsciously require this internally produced chemical to feel "normal," much like a drug addict requires a fix. This need pushes us to re-experience the same feeling so that our body will produce the chemical response it craves.

Freeing ourselves from habitual misery is like breaking an addiction. First, we rely on our mind to help change our actions and feelings. One way we do this is to "think our way into right action." We think about doing something different and that very thought leads us to act in a more desirable way. Either repulsion to the old way or a strong attraction to the new way can sometimes change our behavior. That's great when it works; however, if we continue to feel miserable, there are additional tools that can help us take our thought–action response to a deeper level.

As recurring misery hits, we can train our mind to automatically apply the differentiation questions of the Engineering Problem-Solving Technique. Asking ourselves these simple questions can help us substitute a new, effective pattern for the old, unconscious habit of just sliding into emotional responses and accepting them as they come. Each time misery surfaces, as soon as we notice that our peace and happiness have started to erode, we can ask ourselves specific questions:

1. Is it really a problem?
2. Is it my responsibility to solve it?
3. Can I do anything about it today?
4. Do I really want to solve this?

This helps us logically assess our misery and, hopefully, see it as an illusory problem—something that initially appears as a problem but fades in significance under the light of logical scrutiny. It offers the opportunity to understand that the feeling may seem to be an urgent concern, but the cause of the feeling is not an immediate problem.

If applying these mental tools doesn't relieve the misery, then it's time to add energy from our physical life arena.

The Physical Life Arena and Misery: Act Your Way into Right Thinking

When you first practice these new skills, you may have to *act* your way into *right thinking* instead of trying to *think* your way into *right acting*. This may sound a little confusing, or like a play on words, at first, but it's neither, as you'll soon see.

Sometimes it's possible to change our actions and the mind will follow this new and different course. How do we determine the right action? Hopefully, we will have included a request for guidance while doing the "During the Day" exercise. But also, a few of the tried and true physical acts that help relieve emotional pain also work for misery. Writing a gratitude list, taking a walk, reading uplifting material, exercising, journaling about our feelings, or finding a way to help another person can all help to redirect our thinking. And that is exactly what we need to do.

We perform these physical actions to change the patterns of our thinking, to shift our thought process. We want our directed thoughts, our random thoughts, and our daydreaming thoughts to help us shift our feelings. In that regard, we try to take the physical actions that will propagate the types of thinking that will help us. We select our actions with some wisdom.

For example, repeatedly watching a violent movie or most TV programming may get our mind off of our problems but it won't provide the constructive messages we need right now. At times, numbing our mind might be the only alternative that works to break our cycle of unhealthy thinking; however, it's not as productive over the long term as building new response habits. Perhaps we can make our physical action more helpful by watching programming that makes our mind consider more pleasant alternatives, such as watching a nature channel, daydreaming about a vacation, or watching an inspiring movie that gets us out of our self-driven thoughts. The more intense our misery symptom is, the more we need to select alternatives that do not reinforce our negative patterns.

If applying mental and physical energies fails to provide a solution, we have done everything in our power to change. Now, we turn to our infinite power source, our spiritual relationship.

The Spiritual Relationship

Review your spiritual relationship. Are you putting another person ahead of God ? Are you putting self-will ahead of your spiritual guidance? Has your mind taken control of decisions that should be spiritually guided? Do you *feel* spiritually connected?

Spiritual maintenance is a prerequisite for long-term serenity and happiness. Try to expand and enhance your personal image of God and your concepts of spiritual understanding. Be diligent in doing the daily exercises. Spend time in the morning, during the day, and at night getting in touch with your inner spirit. These actions move you toward the integration of your physical, mental, and spiritual life arenas.

The combination of a spiritually focused mind and spiritually directed willpower create an awesome force that can perform wonders in our life. Of course, they work better if we respond at our first sign of upset feelings, before misery can become imbedded. Any feeling of misery has a starting point, a time when it's a germinating idea, a small, weak voice. It's much easier to eradicate at that point than after it has gained strength and momentum.

Spiritual Engineering provides the process that can move us from despair to happiness and from a life that's mediocre to one of exhilarating joy and adventure, but at times it can seem like a three-step process—two steps forward and one step back. There will be times when we return to misery, when the old patterns overcome our efforts. This is natural and to be expected, so don't be discouraged or frustrated when it happens. As we practice and develop these skills over time, we will notice a significant decrease in the frequency and depth of our recurring misery. We now have a solution. No form or degree of misery can survive the combination of focused mental techniques, physical actions, and spiritual guidance and power. But we still have to do the work.

Go Where the Light Shines: God Has the Flashlight

"When you come to the end of all the light you know, and it's time to step into the darkness of the unknown, faith is knowing that one of two things shall happen: Either you will be given something solid to stand on or you will be taught to fly."

—Edward Teller

I'd stayed on the mountain too late again. The fall twilight was fading and darkness was quickly taking over the shadows, even at our high elevation. I knew a game trail that ran from where I was down to the lower valley. Getting to that point would let me ride Lady, my mare, back to my camp that was just a few miles upriver. Then I wouldn't have to spend a cold night on the mountain with no sleeping bag or gear. I led Lady down the twisting, narrow game path. A canopy of overhanging trees from the heavy forest blocked even the dim light of dusk. My flashlight beam pierced the darkness, illuminating where we could safely walk. With the light, we could avoid the intruding branches and find a way around the rocks and fallen trees. The trail narrowed in places so tightly that we had to force our way through. We slid across some muddy areas and stumbled on a few rocks, but at last we broke out into the valley.

I swung into the saddle and let Lady pick the path from there. I knew that she'd take me right to camp. Riding a great horse in quiet, alone time, entirely at peace and full of wonder at the star-filled night sky, I had an epiphany about what had just happened. I thought about the difference between this short adventure and how, as a child, my mother and I would be walking at night down a country road. She'd sometimes let me have the flashlight to lead the way. I'd always shine it far down the path ahead to see how far I could see. Or I'd keep swinging it from side to side, playing with the light. Mom would say, "Keep the light in the path. We have to see where we are putting our feet."

This time, I used the light differently than when I was a child. I instinctively knew that the trail would be full of turns and obstacles, so I concentrated on shining the light directly where I would place my foot for the next step. This realization gave me a new perception of God and my spiritual journey.

I realized that my experience on that dark trail was similar to the way God seems to work in my life. Sometimes I need direction, guidance about which path to take, to know where I can safely walk. And God has the flashlight. He lights the *exact* spot where I need to place my foot on the very next step. He never illuminates the full path ahead but just the one small place where I must step to make the safest journey. Being human, this is not the kind of answer I like.

I still have a lot of the child in me. It has some good attributes, like endless curiosity, and others that are just plain immature. I want to see every twist and turn that lies ahead; I want to know where the path ends. I want to be able to make my own trail, to go where I want to go instead of following life's natural course. I have the free will to do these things, but if I ignore the path that is illuminated by the light, if I choose to deviate from the way that is marked, I hit obstacles that hurt me. I can take side trails that turn out to be dead ends, and then I have to backtrack. Some ways appear to be easier, but then I hit the boulders and briars. Or I may take a false trail until it disappears and I find out I'm lost.

Life just works out better when I go where the light shines.

I spent much of my life not thinking about God's will or a spiritual path, and there were consequences to my actions. Then I started trying to follow this new direction, to make decisions based on values, on what was right instead of what I wanted at that moment in time. This improved all areas of my life. Although I sincerely wanted to do the right thing, I often had trouble knowing the correct choice. My deeply ingrained patterns of making choices based on self-driven will gave me little idea of how to align with the universal principles. But as I persisted, I discovered a few helpful things:

- The correct choice always demonstrates healthy love.
- The right or wrong of any action is often determined by the motive.
- Like everyone, I have an inner compass to help me find the right path, but it doesn't send e-mails or emblazoned

directions that I can conveniently read. It speaks in whispers and offers gentle, subtle leadings.
- God is a gentleman. He doesn't interrupt or go where He's not invited. If I want to know the right way, I need to ask.
- At times, I may not know what God's will is but I often know what it isn't.

It helps if I can be still, rest in the moment, and make decisions that correspond to this harmonious way of life.

Making Decisions

I sometimes tell people that, when Patricia and I got married, we agreed that she would make all the small, day-to-day decisions and I would make the major ones. This has worked out very well because, in our many years together, we haven't faced a single major decision. She promises to let me know when I need to make one.

In all seriousness, making beneficial decisions is critical to achieving a higher quality of life. We make hundreds of choices that, by themselves, have no impact on our spirituality or integrity. These routine decisions are just part of moving through daily life. Yet, the way we handle those establishes our patterns for making major decisions. We need to become aware that some of these seemingly innocent choices contribute to our emotional unrest.

When we make a conscious or unconscious decision that is actuated by an unhealthy motive, we may experience slight feelings of unease or discontent. We ignore or bury these uncomfortable feelings and move on. Each time we do this is like putting a rock in our pocket. At some point, the cumulative weight will cause a problem and we will be totally unaware of our contribution to the problem. (Our pockets can only stand so much weight until they tear open.) That's why it is important to make beneficial *conscious* choices. Let's look at a few examples of routine choices.

Choosing to watch a football game instead of mowing the lawn probably won't cause me any problems. I may get to enjoy the game with friends, participate in a little socializing, and have a fun day. There's nothing wrong with that. But even here, I have to make sure that this is not part of a hidden pattern of avoiding work in order to have fun. A one-time choice may be beneficial if it is not part of the habit of engaging in self-indulgence at the expense of fulfilling responsibility.

Suppose I choose to have steak for dinner instead of pizza. There's nothing important there, right? However, if I choose the steak because I want to impress you with my ability to afford it, or for some other unhealthy motive, that choice could, again, be part of a pattern that can cause me trouble.

Now, let's say that my boss asked me to do some research for a project and deliver it to her Wednesday afternoon, but I got busy and forgot about it. Wednesday morning she asks how it's coming along. I tell her that I had some real challenges getting the information, that a vendor did not get back to me the way he promised, but I will have the research for her by Thursday morning. I let everything else go, work through lunch, continue working all afternoon, and still have to stay two extra hours. I finally get it done and I feel good. After all, I met my responsibility. My boss didn't know that I had forgotten the work, so it didn't reflect poorly on me. However, *Spiritual Engineering* asks us to consider a different view.

This example, although it might seem unimportant, highlights a number of potential concerns. First of all, why did I forget the initial assignment? Did I fail to write myself a reminder note? Did I get distracted by an upcoming social event and simply forget about something more important? Did I procrastinate, thinking I could do it later? Why did I lie when I was asked how the assignment was coming? Could I have just answered that I would have it Thursday morning and let it go at that? Why did I have to make up a story that wasn't true?

I faced no outward consequence for my wrong action; I seemed to get away with it. But deep inside of me, another set of consequences may emerge. I might feel slightly tense and uneasy from the fear or guilt associated with this action. This may not be an overwhelming sense of wrongdoing but only a subtle feeling of discomfort. This, in turn, may make me short and uncaring with a fellow worker, or lead me to react in anger at some trivial thing that was done by a family member.

Most of the choices we make every day may seem inconsequential. However, the ways we handle them can be part of establishing our patterns for making major decisions, the choices that can change the direction of our lives. We don't need to overwork the process of evaluating these minor options, but we should try to become aware of such choices instead of allowing our unconscious, automatic response system make them for us.

As we encounter decisions we want or need to make, we might pause and ask our self a few questions, such as:

- Is it right or is it wrong?
- Am I doing this to fill my inner void?
- Is this a healthy or unhealthy "hole" filler?
- Is my motive selfish, self-righteous, self-centered, or fearful? Or is it based on love and service?
- Will this choice advance or retard my spiritual growth?
- Does it align with my core values?

Even in this part of our decision-making process, we do not relinquish the practical tools we have. We continue to apply pro-and-con lists, decision trees, models, checklists, or other tools when they're useful. These physical and mental techniques can help clarify our assessment. Again, using three resources, three forms of energy, helps us find and implement the best solution more effectively than just using one or two.

I mentioned that Patricia and I have a God chair at our table as a physical reminder to include the spiritual aspect in our decision-making and conflict resolutions. Requesting guidance in prayer and meditation also helps. Making an effort to incorporate this sacred connection automatically improves our process and outcome.

Guidance often comes in the form of tender tugs, to take a certain step or to go in a certain direction. Sometimes they arise as thoughts, but they can also emerge as feelings. This has presented a twofold challenge for me.

First, I still have trouble differentiating these inspirations from the mental self-talk that is generated by my ego. I have made some dumb mistakes, thinking I was following an inner leading. I am slowly learning to make fewer such errors. Talking this over with someone who is traveling the same path has been a tremendous help. Also, when I seek inner guidance, it helps to be as empty of preconceived preferences as I can be. I may have to pray for open-mindedness and receptivity.

Then when it comes to accepting that a feeling can act as guidance, I've had other challenges. All my life I have been a practical, logic-driven man, so acknowledging that a feeling may prove more correct than my thinking has not been easy. But I cannot argue with experience and results. Sometimes my inner spirit of truth seems to generate a slight foreboding feeling that I should not make this choice or take this action; there can be a wisp of heaviness that develops when I consider certain options.

At other times I have felt a resonance, an inner certainty that moving in a particular direction is right, or that what I have just thought or discovered is the truth. Even with the mistakes I've made, trying to respond to this indwelling guide has yielded significantly better choices and consequences than depending solely on my mind. Interestingly, I have come to believe that many women are endowed with an inherent ability to recognize these personal leadings that I must work so hard to develop and maintain.

Making better decisions, in turn, means that we will avoid many of the difficulties we used to encounter. As we upgrade our choices using these tools, our quality of life increases proportionally. We are less likely to find ourselves in a position where we can be hurt. We learn to recognize misery symptoms earlier and take action to minimize the discomfort. But we still experience uncertainty, adversity, blah days, challenges in relationships, and temporary upset feelings. Generally, these occur for two reasons.

First, life just keeps throwing mud balls at us. Random acts of nature still occur and bring hardship into our lives. We will encounter people who base their lives on self-centered motives, who try to manipulate, take advantage of, or control us. Our responses to those things determine whether these teachers will add to or subtract from our evolving growth.

Second, practicing these principles—replacing old patterns with a new model for living—is progressive. Each decision–action sequence that is based on love and service strengthens our newly evolving patterns. However, our old patterns of making self-will decisions do not just wither and die. They lie dormant, ready to sprout whenever they're watered by wrong motives or bad decisions.

Every choice we face in life, small or large, conscious or unconscious, offers an opportunity to go the new way or the old way, to build and strengthen our new patterns or to resurrect our old ones. Even the choices we make that are obvious mistakes, resulting in misery and suffering can have value if we learn from them. We often gain wisdom only by experiencing tribulation.

God might live in eternity, as some people say, but I'm quite sure he works in the present moment, in the exact minute or second I reside at any given time. Eternity presents a nebulous, impossible-to-imagine concept, but knowing what I have to do right now is extremely important. Remaining focused on the action I need to take *this very instant* to best follow the natural order, knowing where I need to put my foot right now to keep from stumbling and hurting myself, is the key to living an efficient life. It's going with the flow, going down the open, easy trail instead of fighting through the barriers. Right now—this minute, this second—is where spiritual power actually functions.

Again, the problem is all in my mind. My mind is the only part of me that travels in time, despite what Star Trek or science fiction writers tell us. My body stays rooted in the exact place and time it is. Yet on its own accord, my mind journeys into the past and finds regrets, should have's, and resentments; or it goes into the future to collect worry, fear, and anxiety. Then this magical mind brings these feelings back to the present time to torture me. Years of practice make this action into a powerfully entrenched pattern that is difficult to change. But now I have physical, mental, and spiritual resources available to help.

I can look at my feet.

When I find that a misery symptom is interfering with my peace of mind, focusing my attention on my feet brings my mind back to the present moment. This may sound silly, but it works. I look at my feet and mentally acknowledge that my mind has again drifted into the past or future. I realize that it's just reverting to old behavior and I must bring it back to the present moment. I say a quick prayer to my indwelling energy to help me live in the moment, and I direct my mind to focus on my feet. I look at them and realize that they are solidly planted, firmly anchored in the *now*, the only moment in time that has any real meaning. Then I try to think something along the lines of: "Right now, this very moment, everything is okay. I'm alive, I'm breathing, and I'm in pretty good shape. Things could be worse. I need to be grateful for what I have instead of worrying about what I don't have. At this very moment—right here and right now, where my feet are—I am all right."

In our morning prayer, we can ask God to increase our awareness of when our mind starts its time travel and ask him to help us take a positive action as soon as we realize that is happening. We may ask for help in remembering to look at our feet. We may read a few lines in a meditation book, or we may listen to an uplifting CD to keep our mind in the moment.

Walking my spiritual path has enhanced my understanding of certain words and concepts. Words that used to have a negative connotation for me now seem okay, even attractive at times, like the idea of surrender. From the time I was little I was taught to never surrender, to never give up. I was read *The Little Engine That Could*, a famous children's story about a very small engine that overcame insurmountable odds because he just kept trying and saying, "I think I can, I think I can." And I remember hearing the song "High Hopes" about the ram that kept butting the dam with his head in order to break the dam. It took me quite a while to learn that even such virtuous ideas must be tempered with wisdom.

That do-or-die attitude formed one of my deeply entrenched patterns. The self-righteous idea of never surrendering kept me drinking alcohol, pursuing unhealthy relationships, and accepting emotional abuse, even after I was aware that those situations were harmful to me. My resistance to surrender almost killed me.

The logic and practice of *Spiritual Engineering* helped me accept that the Eleventh Commandment may not say, "You will never surrender." If I'm doing something that's not working, I need to give up, recognize that it's wrong, and find a better way. If I keep doing the same thing, I'll keep getting the same results. Once that realization pierced my armor against surrender, my resistance started to wane. I began to see that giving up might be a good thing at times. In fact, it might be absolutely necessary, if I am to move forward in life. That awareness opened me up to new ideas and new experiences.

Eventually, I came to wholeheartedly accept the idea of surrender. I actually embraced it. I understood that, without surrender, I could never find happiness or peace. I came to understand that when I surrender there is no struggle; when I give up, I can move on; when I let go, I can grasp what is truly important. As long as my hand clutches what I want, I cannot open it to receive what I need. Contention, anxiety, and misery often occur when I have not surrendered. There is a balance. Experience teaches me what I need to release and when to release it. I can pursue many things actively and passionately; I can strive for great goals and attempt to achieve them; but I must learn to do all things with inner peace and serenity. Only then am I living in the natural order.

The Door to Peace

This surrendering to the idea of surrendering is an example of the progressive nature of acceptance. I did not rush out and embrace the idea of surrender. I bloodied myself many times fighting that giant. My initial insight, solely based on survival, was that I had to surrender in certain areas of my life, even if I hated the idea. Then I began to see that giving up might be beneficial. Finally, I accepted that surrender was an absolute necessity for my peace of mind, and I would not change it even if I could. When I have problems letting go, I ask my inner spiritual power for help: I ask for the willingness to release whatever it is. If I find that I'm still hanging on, I ask for the willingness to be willing.

The Value of a Vessel Is Its Emptiness

Clay is formed into a vessel.
The emptiness bounded by the clay creates the usefulness
of the vessel.
Walls, windows, and doors make boundaries of a room.
The value is its emptiness, not the boundaries.

—Verse 11, Tao Te Ching, Lao Tzu

The *Tao Te Ching* may seem a little abstract for this practical approach to living but engineering problem solving teaches us to accept help from all available sources. The verse above expresses an idea that fits well with many of the universal principles.

If I have a pitcher full of dirty water and I want to serve my tired and thirsty guests, the container is worthless until I empty it, clean it, and refill it with clean water. This simple, easily understood action has many truths that can help us understand our participation in misery and identify at least part of the solution. As long as the pitcher is full of something else, it cannot do what I need it to do. It can occupy space and sit there and look pretty, but it cannot fulfill its intended purpose, which is to receive, hold, and then distribute clean water. It must be emptied before it can be filled.

The walls of the pitcher define its shape and may contain decorations that enhance its beauty. These physical boundaries are what we see and identify as the pitcher. However, the attribute that makes this vessel worth having exists inside its walls. *Its value lies in the emptiness.* This emptiness is an absolute prerequisite before it can hold something more valuable. Likewise, we can never receive the new while we are full of the old.

If I am full of knowing, I cannot learn.
If I am full of physical things, I cannot receive spiritual
insight or power.
If I am full of misery, I cannot accept happiness.
If I am full of myself, there is no room for others.

I can be filled with knowledge but void of wisdom.
I can be filled with facts but not know truth.
I can be filled with action but empty of results.
I can be filled with doing and miss being.

The most valuable teaching is wasted on me unless I become teachable.

Reflecting on this analogy, I see that there are a number of different ways to empty the pitcher and refill it with clean water. As mentioned, I can empty the dirty water, clean the inside walls, fill it with clean water, and be ready to serve my guests. Or, I can run a stream of clean water into the vessel until all of the dirty water has been replaced, but this still leaves the inside somewhat unclean. Cleaning the interior this way requires more time and energy than the first method and cannot get it as clean. Taking this a step further, I can replace the dirty water a single drop at a time. Eventually, I may end up with water to serve, but the guests will likely be long gone. If I want to have a pitcher of clean water, obviously some methods are more effective than others. If I want to rid myself of harmful patterns and fulfill my potential, the same logic will apply.

Meditation: More than the Sound of Silence

Meditation has not come easily to me.

I have a mind that absolutely refuses to be quiet. For years this tantalizing, tormenting, trying thinker controlled my life. Like a child who has run unchecked from birth, it constantly fights against slowing down, against relinquishing its freedom and its power. My mind is certain that it has a 24/7 full-time job of generating thoughts. It feels like a failure unless it can think something that gets my attention. So it shoots off thoughts like a Fourth of July fireworks display, hoping that one of them will spark some interest. My mind avoids quiet and hates discipline. In fact, you might say it has a mind of its own.

I'm pretty sure that when my mind hears the word meditation or find this idea sneaking into my thought stream; it lets out a belly laugh: "Go ahead. Try it and see what I do." But in spite of this active resistance and totally uncooperative force, I have been able to learn to meditate. (A little bit, sometimes.) Meditation helps me to discipline and train my unruly mind. I struggled with meditation for a long time, but I can share what finally worked for me. If you want to take control of your mind, meditation can be a powerful ally.

First of all, if you don't have a daily meditation book by this time, please get one. Go to a bookstore and browse through a few of them. Read some random selections and find one that appeals to you. Develop a new habit of starting each day in quiet communion with your inner spirit presence, perhaps using the guidelines in the "Starting Your Day Exercise," or something similar. Acknowledge that you want to use your mind the way it was designed to be used, that you are making a conscious choice to seek direction in appropriate decisions. Ask for strength and help in doing this. Read the daily thought from your book. Then, turn to one of the two forms of meditation to start retraining your mind.

Contemplative meditation uses direct participation of mental activity, and it often provides a good starting point. In this type of meditation, we read descriptions of spiritual values, concepts, or practices that we'd like to incorporate into our lives. The daily thought that we read might be a good source for this. Or we may use aspirations or affirmations of qualities we want to acquire. Most religious writings, and many unaffiliated writings, contain inspiring verses or prayers that can elevate us. One example is the beautiful serenity prayer:

"God, grant me the serenity to accept the things I cannot change, the courage to change the things I can, and the wisdom to know the difference."

Next, we will reflect on the meaning of specific words and of each line that we've read. Perhaps we can ask ourselves questions with quiet pauses between each query. Why ask God to *grant* this? Why use that word? What are the things I cannot change? Why would I want to accept them? Would accepting them cease my inner struggle and make life easier? What things can I change? Why am I asking God to grant me courage? Don't I have enough courage of my own? Am I willing to make these changes? What blocks me from wanting to change? Am I afraid? I'm asking God to grant the *wisdom to know the difference,* but how does this apply to the choices I'm faced with right now? What is wisdom? What wise or unwise past choices might guide me in making this decision? Which alternative might reflect more wisdom?

We try to see how the substance of that request might enhance our life. We spend a few moments contrasting our request for serenity, courage, and wisdom with our current outlook or action, envisioning how we can practice this. We reflect on how these attributes would improve our attitude and behavior. We try to develop an appreciation of this higher way of being, and we foster a desire to make it a part of our daily life.

Quiet meditation utilizes a different technique, but it accomplishes the same objective. We use quiet meditation to help us calm our overactive mind so we can sit in silence and access the inner power that fills our entire being with peace, strength, and purpose. There are a number of practices that can help with this. They range from a variety of well-established Eastern meditations to methods adapted to our Western Judeo-Christian heritage. Each practice uses different tools to help us break our old patterns of constant mental self-talk and guide us to the place of inner quiescence, a place of empty receptivity. Quiet meditation is a method of achieving the emptiness that is mentioned in the Tao Te Ching. Investigate different approaches until you find the one that works best for you.

One example of a Western meditation is the Centering Prayer method espoused by Father Thomas Keating in his book *Open Mind, Open Heart* (Continuum Press, New York). This technique has been helpful to me. It explained why my progress often seemed begrudgingly slow, and it gave me an opportunity to achieve a little quiet meditation when nothing else seemed to work. After a few years of trying it persistently, I can now get a few seconds and sometimes even a few minutes, of quiet time out of my attempts. I consider this a great success. I have experienced a few "aha" moments and insights, but the real benefits show in my progressively more peaceful response to life. Centering Prayer is one more tool that can move us toward personality integration—allowing our mind to gradually become directed by our inner spirit guide.

Recognize Your Teachers

A bed of beautiful roses still has thorns. Our attempts to lead a spiritual life will not turn everyone we meet into a loving, caring individual. Some people may challenge our happiness and serenity. Tools like meditation can help us deal with people and minimize the degree to which we allow them to affect our inner life. Paradoxically, the people who cause us the most trouble often end up contributing the most value to our life because they spur us on in our growth.

I've been a doer, an action person, all of my life, which has made it difficult to learn patience. I finally came to a startling realization about that attribute: I had learned more about patience from the people I thought were jerks, who were impediments to my happiness at that time, than I ever learned from a priest, rabbi, or spiritual guru. I may learn the theory and benefits of patience from these teachings, but I learn the applications of patience in daily living. And the people who teach me are the very same ones who frustrate the living daylights out of me. In other words, the men and women who irritate me the most are my real teachers.

I've realized over time that this holds true for many of the positive attributes I want to develop in my life: love, tolerance, forgiveness, and so on. My progress *requires* that I face situations and people that make it difficult to practice those attributes. The more difficult the lesson—the harder it is to exhibit those qualities in a given situation—the greater the resulting progress will be. A few times I've managed to appreciate this view of irksome teachers while they were teaching me. I feel almost euphoric when I can change from being irritated by someone to appreciating him as one of my teachers *in the very moment that the situation is occurring*. This almost instantaneous change in my perception, understanding, and feelings shifts my attitude dramatically.

It seems that there's an almost endless supply of these teachers. That's a scary thought, but it's also a good thing. Once I committed to this spiritual journey, I noticed that the universe unleashes all kinds of help. Not all of its assistance is the kind I might choose. Somehow these people appear in my life, in combination with the wise ministers, to teach me whatever lesson I need at that time. This is a twist on the old adage that "When the pupil is ready, the teacher will appear." But I've noticed that, whenever I am ready to grow in a certain area, the teachers seem to crawl out of the morass of humanity, and they keep showing up in my life until I get the lesson.

This abundance of teachers also means that I can't avoid learning the lesson that each one is supposed to give me. If I revert to old behavior or try to skip the lesson, another teacher will be waiting around the corner. Accepting this fact makes it easier to apply the tools, learn the lesson, be grateful to my teacher, and find peace again.

With that said, spiritual readings and reminders can be of great help in facing those challenges. Below is one from *The Urantia Book* that helped me work through a very trying lesson about tolerance:

> If some one irritates you, causes you feelings of resentment, you should sympathetically seek to discern his viewpoint, his reasons for such objectionable conduct. If once you

understand your neighbor, you will become tolerant and this tolerance will grow into friendship and ripen into love.

In the mind's eye conjure up a picture of one of your primitive ancestors of cave-dwelling times—a short, misshapen, filthy, snarling hulk of a man standing, legs spread, club upraised, breathing hate and animosity as he looks fiercely straight ahead. Such a picture hardly depicts the divine dignity of man. But allow us to enlarge the picture. In front of this animated human crouches a saber-tooth tiger ready to pounce. Behind him a woman and two children. Immediately you recognize that such a picture stands for much that is fine and noble in the human race, but the man is the same in both pictures. Only in the second sketch you are favored with a widened horizon. You therein discern the motivation of this evolving mortal. His attitude becomes praiseworthy because you understand him. If only you could fathom the motives of your associates, how much better you would understand them. If you could only know your fellows, you would eventually fall in love with them.

You cannot truly love your fellows by a mere act of the will. Love is only born of thoroughgoing understanding of your neighbor's motives and sentiments. It is not so important to love all men today, as it is that each day you learn to love one more human being. If each day or each week you achieve an understanding of one more of your fellows, and if this is the limit of your ability, then you are certainly socializing and truly spiritualizing your personality.

When, in the throes of conflict, we can step back and acknowledge that there may be a saber-toothed tiger in the other person's life and that we may not be able to see or understand this tiger, we are making progress. Those who feel loved act lovingly; those who feel fearful act defensively. Everyone can be our teacher.

Who has caused you contention lately? What were you supposed to learn? Did you struggle against learning? Did you finally get the lesson or will it have to be repeated?

We live in a complex, fast-paced, stress-filled world—on the outside. However, we can choose whether our inner life will follow this pattern or pursue more fulfilling goals. By now we know that our inner life is vastly more significant than the outer one. Developing spiritual strength is like developing physical strength: we have to exercise, practice, and learn to use every skill and tool available.

Spiritual Engineering emphasizes some important actions that contribute to our inner life: building our relationships, learning to love our self and others, following the natural order, striving for personality unification, and stretching beyond our self-directed life. Happiness, serenity, and joy—all of the things we might ever want in life—are simply by-products of integrating these actions into our lives. This logical technique offers specific and practical guidelines to accomplish each one of those actions. It directs us to access additional energy from our inner divine source; it helps us train our mind to be a friend instead of an enemy; it teaches us to make better decisions. Taking appropriate actions vastly improves our quality of life. We begin to see that our feelings and relationships follow the same inexorable rules of cause and effect that control the physical world. Some of the mystery is gone.

This human/spiritual journey is about progress. At least that's my experience. I'll never get to where I think I should be and need to accept that as a feature of growth. Even after years of practice, I can still make unbelievable mistakes, or say things I regret. However, these tools help me extract the best from any situation.

Results: Using the Tools

"Good judgment comes from experience, and experience comes from bad judgment."

—Barry LePatner

I was lying on my back in the remote wilderness, looking up at gathering clouds in a deep blue sky, trying to catch my breath, wondering if I'd get out of there alive. I knew my injuries were bad. I couldn't get to my feet—I could barely get to my knees. My back or hips were damaged; something was broken. I was spitting up blood, so I knew I probably also had internal injuries. I was alone. No one knew where I was, and I was miles from help.

Bucked from the horse after he had planted the saddle horn inches deep into my groin, I'd landed with the small of my back directly on a rocky rise in the hard ground. Every time I tried to get up, the pain hit so hard that it took my breath away like a blow to the stomach. I couldn't pass out or I'd be in even worse trouble.

I suddenly realized that I had made some terrible decisions that landed me here. I'd also ignored inner warnings that could have prevented this situation. I'd gotten caught up in self-driven will yet again, after years of practicing how not to do that, and this time I was paying a very dear price. I wouldn't know the full price until I got out of there, but I could indulge in self-recrimination later—if I made it out alive.

Self-Will, Bad Decisions, and Consequences

The Colorado fall of 2008 had crisp cold nights and clear days in the lower elevations, with the forecast calling for snow above ten thousand feet—dream weather for someone who loves the high country, horses, and solitude. Although I didn't know the Colorado Rockies well, I had ridden the wilderness areas of Wyoming with my horses and mules, spending days and weeks by myself. I knew that going alone into these remote areas increased the risk of trouble, but I valued the seclusion, the chance to experience raw nature, and the opportunity to meditate and strengthen my spiritual relationship.

I had decided to take a week off to go elk hunting. For weeks I planned every detail, arranging to rent a horse because I had sold mine when I left Wyoming. I hadn't done this for years and I eagerly anticipated getting back on a horse and riding the high country. My wife, Patricia, knew of my experience with horses and the wilderness. But about two weeks before the departure, she mentioned that she had a bad feeling about this trip, asking if I really thought it was the right thing to do. With my strong desire and past experience, I discounted her apprehension. Later on, when I reviewed what I might have done differently to avoid this near-catastrophe, I realized that that was my *second mistake and first intuitive warning flag.*

Two days before I left, Patricia and I were reviewing exactly where I was going and my scheduled time to come out of the wilderness after six days. As we talked, I mentioned that I had a bad feeling in my gut about this trip. If I could have changed it easily, I would have. But I had vacation time scheduled, I'd rented and paid for a horse, and I had bought a bunch of stuff for the trip. I had cleaned and packed all my tack and camping gear. Canceling would be a hassle and a lot of wasted effort and expense.

Besides, I really wanted to go.

Again, my desire plus my extensive experience overrode the slight nudge of uneasiness. *Third mistake and second intuitive warning flag.* Patricia said, "Promise me you'll take care of yourself and come back." I promised without a second thought. Leaving home, I drove four hours into the mountains. I went to the end of the four-wheel-drive trail and set up camp at a place that was 10,500 feet above sea level. That afternoon, the dude ranch delivered my horse—a strong gelding at sixteen hands, dark gray with a white face and three white stockings.

The next morning, I put my saddle on Baldy and adjusted the tack. My back cinch looked a little tight, but I thought it would loosen up as we rode. This cinch can make the horse buck if it's not adjusted correctly. I thought about taking it off. I looked at it again and noticed another dark, heavy feeling that this wasn't a good idea. But, I mentally argued, I've used this back cinch for years and never had any problems. *(Fourth mistake, third intuitive warning flag.)*

I swung into the saddle and rode out to get used to the unfamiliar horse and the surrounding country. A cold front was approaching. The temperature had peaked at thirty-six degrees just before I rode out and the forecast was calling for a low of eighteen degrees that night. Heading deeper into the mountains and nearing the wilderness area, we rode gently, the horse and I establishing our communication. I was neck reining, backing up, stopping, standing, and so on. Everything was going well.

I moved Baldy to a canter and he just exploded. His first buck took me by surprise, lifting me out of the saddle, but I managed to hold on. While I was coming back down, he bucked high and hard again. This time I felt the saddle horn bury deep into my groin. I still hung on—the breath completely knocked out of me. Baldy went straight up the third time, kicking high with his back feet. I flew off. I landed across a ditch on the small of my back, looking up to see if the horse was going to land on me or stomp me, but I heard him gallop away. I lay there trying to catch my breath and see how badly I was injured.

It was bad.

I rolled off of my back and tried to get to my knees. The pain hit hard and brought tears to my eyes, stopping me before I was halfway up. I tried again but I still couldn't get up. I caught my breath and prayed for help that I could just get to my knees. After three tries, I made it. I felt my lower back and legs but I couldn't feel any obvious fractures. I tried to stand, but again the knifelike pain in my back almost made me pass out. I'd get partway up and the sky would start spinning.

Still on my hands and knees, I assessed my situation.

I was alone. There was no cell phone signal in that remote area. There were no other campers within miles and I had little chance of being found if I stayed where I had fallen. The freezing night temperatures plus the wind-chill would bring even more danger. I had suffered severe hypothermia once before so I well knew that risk. My emergency pack with waterproof matches, flashlight, space blanket, and fire starters was still around my waist, but it would only be useful if I could walk.

I tried to still my breath and be calm. I asked God to help me keep a clear mind, to stay conscious and make the best decision for the situation, and find the strength to do whatever I needed to do. I thanked Him for all of the wonderful blessings I had in my life. I kept remembering my promise to Patricia that I'd return, that nothing would stop me from coming back. I had to get back to my tent and sleeping bag. It was the only place where I might be able to survive the night and a few more days until other hunters came by. My camp was about a mile away. I knew that, if I could get to that point, I might get help, hopefully within a day or so.

But I had to walk or crawl that mile back to camp.

I forced myself to get up, moving through the pain, but then, I couldn't take a single step. My right leg wouldn't move. I had to reach down with my hands, lift it up a little, and move it forward a few inches. Then I'd step out another three to four inches with the left one. After I got them moving, I could lift them one to two inches high and make a few steps before I had to stop.

I'd count the steps, trying to do ten steps between each stop but usually managing less. I knew the principle of living one day at a time, of making one step at a time, but now I was willing to settle for just inches at a time and be grateful for that.

Five steps, stop; catch my breath, make myself realize that, if I did not start again, I could die here; ten steps, stop, catch my breath, pray, tell myself that the pain could slow me down and drain my energy, but it could not stop me unless I let it. Eight steps this time, then fourteen steps, tears rolling down my face, thinking this is impossible—then remembering my promise to Patty—forcing myself forward one more time. I stumbled over a rock and almost went down, the pain wrenching the breath and more tears out of me. My hands on my knees, gasping, forcing myself to stay conscious, I had a fleeting thought that I couldn't make it. Suddenly my years of spiritual practice took over. In the last twenty-eight years I had moved from an agnostic, self-sufficient state of living to that place of absolute certainty of the existence of God and the spiritual force dwelling within me. Peace and serenity returned.

Over and over I repeated this—two hundred, three hundred times or more? I could finally see my camp and SUV. I knew that I couldn't get myself into the vehicle and drive, but it had also seemed impossible that I could have made it this far. I needed to get to my sleeping bag in case I had to wait through the night. Looking at the rocks, broken wood and tall grass that was blocking my path to camp, I knew I'd fall if I tried to trudge through all of that. I got down on my hands and knees and crawled the last two hundred yards.

I rested on my sleeping bag and started feeling drowsy, but I knew that I couldn't fall asleep. If a truck came by, I wouldn't be able to get to where anyone could see me in time. So I crawled to where I could see the road, vomiting blood on the way. I lay there thanking God that I had made it this far, thanking Him for an absolutely awesome experience on this planet. I knew without a doubt that, if my life ended that night, I was one of the most blessed people on earth.

There was no question, I definitely wanted more time to live on this planet. Miss Patty and I share an extraordinary relationship, and we still had many people to help, but I knew those things were out of my control.

I was not the least bit afraid. That was amazing. Fear had dominated so much of my life—fear of what other people thought or said about me, fear of making mistakes, fear of getting caught in my little white lies, fear of not having enough money, fear of what might happen in the future. But now, I could walk no further. I was spitting up blood. There was no one else within miles, and I knew that I might not get out alive—yet I felt no fear. What a magnificent transformation!

Clouds had gathered and started spewing snow, a reminder of the oncoming cold. I lay there for a couple of hours, fighting the tendency to pass out. Then I heard a truck approaching. I tried to wave the people down, yelling as loudly as I could, which was only a feeble cry. The truck kept going up the trail until it was out of sight. Then I heard it stop and back up. It turned around and came down the broken trail to my camp. A man leaned out the passenger window and asked if I was all right. With my voice breaking and tears of gratitude streaming down my face, I could barely answer, but I managed to croak that I needed help.

They got me on a Life Flight to a local trauma unit. My pelvis was severely broken and had split open with a two-inch-wide separation. I also had a slight fracture on my right hip. The attending physician said that twenty percent of breaks like that are fatal. They can cut or perforate arteries located near the break, and any movement greatly increased this risk. He also commented that I must have had a guardian angel looking after me to walk and crawl that distance without puncturing an artery and being able to withstand the pain without losing consciousness or going into shock.

I had called my wife while I was in transit. Her reaction demonstrated her growth from using the these techniques. Patricia, with her Latino heritage, has merged her wonderfully passionate, volatile, loving, dreaming, and excitable attributes with these practical down-to-earth practices. As we spoke, she realized that this had been a narrow escape for me and that I was very fortunate to have gotten out of the wilderness alive. After we hung up, she immediately got on her knees and thanked God I was alive. She asked her inner spirit to guide her mind and help her stay calm so she would take the best actions. After spending a few minutes quieting her mind, she arranged for a close friend to meet her, got directions to the hospital, and then drove to meet me. In all of this, she remained calm, poised, and free of fear.

Evaluating Mistakes

I've spent many years developing and practicing these principles with unbelievable results. They have completely transformed and improved my life. Yet, no matter how long I've done this or how dedicated I've become, there are still times when my old pattern of self-directed will reasserts itself and leads me into making decisions that hurt myself and others. It seems like, while I'm praying, meditating, and serving others, my self-will is doing pushups—staying strong and in shape—just waiting for an opportunity to take control again. When this happens, I can berate myself for failing, or I can seize the opportunity to see how I can improve. I can focus on the dark spot on the windshield, or I can see that the whole windshield looks pretty good.

My recent misadventure demonstrates three main things: mistakes that were motivated by self-will, the reality and significance of intuitive leadings, and the awesome spiritual power that's available in living this way of life. I've pointed out some of the mistakes I made in that process, but if you've noticed, the one that started that sequence of events wasn't emphasized. This first error occurred when I neglected to use the decision-making tools to decide whether or not I should make that trip. I didn't look at my motivation for the escapade—was I mired in self-will or was I asking to be spiritually guided?

If I had done that, there's a chance, albeit a small one, that I might have changed the outcome. Had I stopped to honestly check my motives, I may have become aware that my old pattern of self-righteousness was preventing a healthy evaluation. I might have noticed that I had not given fair consideration to Patricia and another friend when they questioned the advisability of my going alone. I may have seen that I quickly rationalized their concerns as insignificant by reminding them, and myself, that I had spent many days riding alone in wilderness areas with horses and pack mules, with very few problems. Of course, at this time, I was quite a few years older, riding a horse I had never been on, and venturing into unfamiliar wilderness country.

The fact remains that I ignored a basic principle by which I try to live and I paid the price, all because of what *I wanted to do*. And I made additional mistakes by ignoring the warning flags that offered opportunities to avoid the upcoming hardship.

Warning Flags and Lessons

The practical results I've experienced from following this path have opened my mind to other possibilities as well. Specifically, I've come to believe in what are commonly called "gut feelings." These inner indicators can emerge as a slightly apprehensive feeling, like something is wrong, in the pit of my stomach, or they can appear as a feeling that something is intrinsically safe or correct. In hindsight, I've had these all my life, but I ignored them. As a pragmatic engineer, they didn't fit into my view of the world. However, the more I paid attention to them, the more I became convinced that these subtle signals, at times, actually did predict either impending trouble or a favorable outcome. I can't quantify or measure these intuitive urges, but they definitely do exist.

The power of intuition comes from the subliminal processing of all of our mentally submerged historical data, experiences, and sensory input. In other words, our unconscious mind sees what is happening in the present moment, relates this to every detail of every experience we have ever had, correlates all of this input and then processes this information. The conclusion to all of this activity is communicated through an emotional response—a gut feeling—about what our decision should be. These are feelings as opposed to thoughts. They are easy to ignore, especially by those of us who are not very tuned in to our feelings.

Three specific occurrences of these gut feelings occurred in this self-will-driven adventure:

1. Patricia told me of her bad feeling about the trip.
2. I told her that I had a bad feeling about this trip but stubbornly justified my decision to go.
3. When looking at the saddled horse, I had a premonition that the back cinch may be a mistake. Later investigation showed that this likely spooked the horse and directly caused the accident.

These feelings did not manifest as an overwhelming sense of impending doom. They appeared as a slight foreboding, a subtle heaviness, and an uneasy feeling in the pit of my stomach. If I had paid attention to any one of those gut feelings, I would have avoided the accident.

Results

I made mistakes and I reaped the consequences. My power of choice, driven by self-will and strong desires, resulted in some bad decisions. However, the *Spiritual Engineering* tools produced unbelievable results when I finally used them. I had internal injuries and a severely broken pelvis that caused excruciating pain. Yet I was able to walk and crawl back to my camp. An adrenaline rush and determination helped, but prayer and access to my inner source of spiritual energy played a significant role.

I asked for help to do the next thing I had to do, to not pass out while doing it, to have the strength to work through the pain and keep my consciousness, and to be able to concentrate on what had to be done. I could not get to my knees; I prayed and made it. Pain stopped my attempts to rise to my feet, almost making me pass out. I prayed and got to my feet. Time after time pain blocked my efforts to walk, but prayer helped me walk through the pain.

I had total peace of mind from the time I laid on my back in the ditch to the time I arrived at the hospital. Prayer brought me the "peace that surpasses all understanding."

A number of physicians told me I was extremely fortunate that I didn't puncture an artery and bleed to death. They also said they were amazed that I could endure that amount of pain and walk with such a severe fracture. What was it that kept me from going into shock or passing out from the pain? What protected me from puncturing an artery? Was it blind luck, good fortune, or spiritual help?

Also, the men who rescued me had not intended to come that way. They had planned to take a different route, the same one they had traveled the last three years. The driver said that, when he arrived at the intersection of the road where they found me, *he suddenly had a feeling he should go that way.*

How can so many fortuitous turns of events be explained by mere luck or coincidence?

Obviously, trying to lead a life according to the natural order, with an emphasis on practical spirituality, does not preclude accidents or the consequences of making poor decisions or the kinds of suffering that come from random acts of nature. It's not a miraculous umbrella that negates the laws of the universe and protects us from all adversity, but it does offer a quality of life that many of us find extremely desirable.

We will all live until we die. That may sound simplistic, but let's consider it for a moment. Many of us will spend seventy, eighty, or more years on this planet. At the end of our life, how will we judge whether or not it was worth it? Will we add up the things we have accumulated or how much money we made? There's never a U-Haul in a funeral procession: we can't take any of those things with us.

If we have a chance to reflect on our life immediately before we leave this third rock from the sun, we'll probably experience something like I did lying there broken and cold, waiting for someone to save me. The important things at that moment will be the quality of our experiences, our relationships, our personal growth, and our contributions to others.

If we want to extract the maximum happiness and peace of mind from our life, the time to start is now—right now, this very moment. Remember, if nothing changes, *nothing changes*. Each of us must choose: am I going to procrastinate, or am I going to take action now?

We can ask ourselves: Is it my fate to struggle and merely survive? Do I accept misery as a necessary part of life? Do I endure mediocre relationships while I'm dreaming of what might be? Or, can I find a way of life that provides a framework for extraordinary relationships? Is there a process that can actually help me to solve the challenges of living—one that teaches me how to be happy and enjoy peace, even as I'm facing the adversities that life can present?

Spiritual Engineering offers a way to experience those things.

It's not the only answer, and it does take some work. Transforming your life requires effort and direction. I recommend that you start with the foundation: develop your personal spirituality. Learn to love yourself. Eventually, you will be able to apply these skills in all areas of your life.

Then you will have joined what Abraham Maslow called "the apex of human development," that one percent of humanity that develops skills to help them get the absolute most out of life. You will have resurrected yourself from the ashes of your past and joined the Phoenix People.